Murphy's Law

MURPHY'S LAW

A biography of Alex Murphy

BRIAN CLARKE

HEINEMANN KINGSWOOD

Heinemann Kingswood
Michelin House, 81 Fulham Road, London SW3 6RB

LONDON MELBOURNE AUCKLAND

First published 1988
ISBN 0 434 98154 0

Photoset in Linotron Sabon by
Deltatype Ltd, Ellesmere Port
Printed and bound in Great Britain by
Redwood Burn Ltd, Trowbridge, Wiltshire

Contents

List of Illustrations

Acknowledgements

The writing of this book would not have been possible without the generous help given me by my colleague Stuart Pyke, by John Clegg, a director of St Helens RLFC, and by David Howes, the Rugby Football League's public relations officer.

I must also take this opportunity to thank Alice and Alex Murphy for the immense amount of time they have given me in my quest for information; all the players, directors and journalists, who have helped me at various stages of the book's progress; and Derek Wyatt and Tony Pocock whose advice I have found invaluable. I should also like to extend a special word of thanks to the staff of the public libraries in Leigh, Salford, St Helens, Warrington and Wigan for the quite exceptional courtesy they have always shown me.

All the photographs in this book, except four, have been reproduced by kind permission of the Andrew Varley Picture Agency. The exceptions are no. 3 from the Provincial Press Agency, Southport; no. 4 from Geoff Williams, St Helens; no. 8 from the *St Helens Reporter*; and no. 10 from the *County Press*, Wigan.

Brian Clarke

1
Thatto Heath

Alexander James Murphy was born on 22 April 1939 in Thatto Heath, a working-class district of St Helens. He has always been a rebel, with or without a cause. It is a role he has never stopped playing and one that has sustained his critics throughout his career. His straight-talking approach has often infuriated his friends, fuelled his critics and left him exposed to the charge of not caring. But Murphy does care – and most passionately – about his rugby. On the field of play he always met danger head on. The world's outstanding scrum-half believed that his strength, allied to a jaguar's pace, would take him clear of trouble; only rarely did it fail him.

Blessed with natural ability, Murphy had no arduous climb to the top. From his early competitive days at school he simply leapt from one pinnacle to another. Captain of his school's junior and senior teams before he was twelve, a regular member of St Helens Town and Lancashire schoolboy teams at fourteen, he was the proverbial 'boy wonder' on the rugby field. Signed by St Helens at midnight on his sixteenth birthday, he blazed a trail to Australia and New Zealand while still a teenager and established a world reputation before he was twenty-one.

Man and boy, Murphy has bathed in the sunshine of adulation which has often blurred his vision and left him accused of being a 'big head' and a 'know-all'. Murphy takes these criticisms on the chin: 'I've always believed in speaking my mind and telling people straight what I think.' His reponses are more impulsive than thoughtful but tempered with the extrovert's generous nature. He can be witty, charming, warm-hearted and downright, unthinkingly rude. He is a man who stirs great anger but who commands fierce loyalties especially where Rugby League is concerned. His is a nature that has made Murphy the dominating personality in world rugby – on and off the field – for more than thirty years.

The three great influences in his formative rugby years were his father James, his headmaster at St Austin's School, Gerry Landers, and his first professional coach, Jim Sullivan, the immortal Welshman of both rugby codes who nurtured Murphy's explosive talent. In nostalgic mood Murphy expresses admiration for the men, though at the time he often thought them harsh and unfair. His father James was a professional who played centre for Warrington and encouraged Murphy in his rugby career each step of the way. His mother, Sarah Alice, had five children to bring up: three girls and two boys – Alex and his elder brother Billy. The small council home at 25 Sunbury Street, Thatto Heath was built on a steep hill, and the family enjoyed few luxuries. 'Bread and jam could make you fat but that hill kept us all in trim,' chuckles Murphy.

His mother remembers that her youngest child loved 'playing around with a ball' almost as soon as he could walk. Brother Billy's talents, on the other hand, developed on the table-tennis table: 'I remember a professional coming to our district to give exhibitions,' Murphy recalls. 'Our Billy played him and licked him by three games to one. My dad was really keen for Billy to become a table-tennis professional after that, but Billy didn't want that. Dad was upset about it at the time because he believed Billy was throwing away his talent so I decided that I would try to make up for it by pleasing my dad and turning professional at rugby.'

Murphy's parents had to work hard with five children to clothe and feed. Nothing was wasted at the Murphy home. Old rags tied together with string became a makeshift rugby ball for Murphy and his friends around hard-up Sunbury Street. 'We played more with a bundle of rags than with anything else in those days. Consequently handling a rugby ball became second nature to all the lads,' Murphy remembers. In those days he was a lad in a hurry. He was off to St Austin's School at 8 a.m. so that he could have an hour in the playground with a rugby or soccer ball before lessons started.

But Murphy's boyhood enthusiasm almost wrecked his rugby career before it had started. 'One morning we were kicking a ball around in the school playground and I tried to be clever. I trapped the ball just as another lad came flying into me with a tackle. His clogs caught me a real blow and I limped into class that morning with my ankle really sore and swelling. Murphy complained but the headmaster, Gerry Landers, was unimpressed and wary of being taken for a ride. Murphy was ordered to remain in his class until the lunch break, when he was allowed to go home, and he remembers the painful walk of one and a half miles to Sunbury Street. But his problems weren't over. 'My dad thought I was making an excuse for playing wag and sent me back to school. Later I had to be taken to hospital and it was discovered that I'd broken my ankle in two places.'

However, despite all the trials and tribulations Murphy enjoyed his schooldays and especially his lessons in drawing and art. But he quickly realized his limitations. 'I was in the 'C' class; and you could say we were not over-bright. I was poor at maths and appalling at spelling, and I realized early on that I was not going to be the Town Clerk when I grew up'.

Garry Landers had always instilled a sense of compassion into the rough and ready boys of St Austin's. They were reminded from time to time that elsewhere in the world there was always someone in real need. The 'waifs and strays' collection to raise money for underprivileged children was one such reminder. But the collection always left Murphy and his friends in 'C' class with a deep sense of inadequacy. 'I remember two lads from Rainhill, one of the 'posh' districts, giving £1 each to one 'waifs and strays' collection,' says Murphy. 'In our class we managed only 2s.6d. between us.' The thought of being second best at collection time had wrankled with Murphy for some time and he constantly thought of ways of correcting the situation. One morning on his way to school he hit on the solution. His mother had given him £2 with instructions to call at the local Co-op on his way home to collect the family's grocery order. It presented Murphy with a golden chance to beat the 'poshies' in the school collection that day.

With his mother's £2 the bait, Murphy proposed to his class-mates that they dig deep into their pockets for the collection. 'We were all poor in 'C' class, but with my mother's £2 and money from the other lads we gave the most to the collection that day. I felt ten foot tall. We were top dogs and got five merit marks and stars for collecting the most. It was great.' But Murphy's joy was shortlived. At home that evening he was unable to convince his mother that he had lost her £2 for the family groceries. 'When she got the truth out of me, my mother dragged me back to school after telling me she was trying to bring up waifs and strays of her own.' At St Austin's Murphy was ordered to reveal the truth of the 'C' class collection to his teacher, Billy Fyldes, with his mother present. Mr Fyldes listened in horror to the tale and Murphy knew he was about to cop it on two fronts. Mr Fyldes handed back Mrs Murphy's £2 and then, when she had left, he gave him six of the best and took away the merit marks and stars the class had been given. 'It taught me a painful lesson, especially about trying to kid my mum,' Murphy says now.

On another occasion the young Murphy fell foul of his grandfather after a display of youthful honesty earned him a tongue-lashing and a clip round the ear. 'Grandad had a horse and cart and used to travel the district selling lettuce and cabbage. He used to give me three pence pocket-money for helping him. I knocked on one door and offered a lady two lettuces. She was going to buy them when I noticed a slug on one of the leaves and pointed to it. She didn't buy the lettuce and when I told my grandad about it he was furious and gave me a real ticking off for not making the sale.'

Murphy had other sidelines for making extra pocket-money. 'I used to take horse-racing bets for the neighbours because I was the fastest runner in the district and could get away if the police arrived on the scene.' He also acted as 'look out' for local men playing the illegal game of pitch and toss. 'The men used to give me tips for watching out for the police for they knew I was the fastest runner in the neighbourhood. Some days I felt like a millionaire.'

All this time, Murphy's father constantly encouraged his youngest son to take his rugby seriously. The two would go to Wilderspool together to watch Warrington's home matches. Murphy senior knew that his son would be able to watch Warrington's international half-back pairing of Gerry Helme and Ray Price, and hoped that their influence would rub off on his son.

Of course father took him also to St Helens especially when the Australian tourists were playing, and the two of them used also to go to Old Trafford when the Australian cricket tourists were playing there. 'My dad liked watching great players in action in any sport. When we watched the Aussie cricketers he told me I could be as good as them at my chosen sport if I was prepared to work hard enough. But I knew I had to convince dad that I was keen enough to play rugby as a career. When mum and dad bought me my first pair of rugby boots and shorts it must have nearly broken them. They had very little money to spare, and I vowed then that I would never let them down.'

There's little doubt that Murphy's father wanted him to join Warrington where injury had ended his own playing career. Indeed, Warrington offered over £1,500 for his son's signature – which would have been a small fortune to the Murphys in those days. 'That money would have made my parents rich, but I told my father that if I couldn't play for my own town team, St Helens, then I wouldn't play for anyone. It's the only time I ever answered my father back.' Murphy later signed for St Helens for the princely sum of £80!

Murphy's mother has clear memories of the time when rugby scouts tried to capture her youngest son's burgeoning talents. 'When Alex was fifteen I went with his father to Warrington to watch him playing his last schoolboy match before leaving school. I remember a rugby scout approaching his father and offering him over a thousand pounds in cash for our Alex if he would sign for his club. But Alex was always headstrong. He told us he would play marbles or kick a can about in the streets if he couldn't play for St Helens. His heart was set on going to Saints.'

Rugby scouts and coaches weren't the only people interested in Murphy as news of his potential spread. Scouts from Liverpool and Everton soccer clubs had already begun making inquiries about him. 'I could have joined Everton,' recalls Murphy. 'But I didn't want to play soccer. It wasn't exciting enough for me. Rugby was my real love in sport.'

Gerry Landers recognized before most that there was something special about Murphy, particularly when he had a rugby ball in his hands, and he proved a powerful influence in developing that quality in his star pupil. On one occasion Landers was holding a team talk for his St Austin's senior team before an important match. He assembled the boys in the cloakroom after school and demanded their attention. When he saw Murphy bending his head as if hiding his face the headmaster was furious. 'Gerry Landers thought I was laughing. He took the towel roll off the wall and cracked me over the shoulders with it. It certainly made me pay attention.'

But if Landers made Murphy feel his disciplinary wrath he also gave him advice and encouragement that was to benefit him throughout his playing career. 'The head drummed into me that passing a rugby ball was like learning how to dance. He told me I had to practise each step and movement until it was perfect. He used to stand me in the school yard and teach me how to pass a ball. I can remember the instructions he shouted at me. "One, two, three left . . . one, two, three right . . . one, two, three forward . . . My pals used to watch and take the mickey. But those hours of learning how to pass a ball helped me tremendously later in my career. I could pass a ball right or left going at speed without even checking my stride. Gerry Landers taught me that, and I was always grateful to him. I knew more about rugby at fourteen than some players know at forty. He taught me how to feed a scrum, where the hooker's feet should be and when to go round the blind side. He said it was an art.'

St Austin's produced a galaxy of stars, with the top professional scouts always at their matches. Inter-school rivalry was so intense, and the standard of schoolboy rugby was so high, that matches could command crowds of over 7,000 – more even than some of the less fashionable professional clubs.

The St Helens Town team was picked by a committee in those days. One of its members was Harry Cook, a deputy headmaster who became the longest-serving chairman in the history of St Helens Rugby League club. An excellent judge of a rugby player, Cook had Murphy in his sights as soon as the youngster's talents came into focus in the Town team. 'I marked him down when he was very young. He was such an outstanding prospect. I told myself, "We must get this Murphy." There were dozens of outstanding young prospects but Alex was the best.'

Cook wasn't the only good judge to think so, Murphy was to underline the point in his first big competitive schoolboy match, playing at the age of twelve for the St Austin's senior team against Central Modern, another local school with much-sought-after young players. A big crowd turned up to watch the two schools compete for a place in the area finals of the *Daily Dispatch* Shield, sponsored by the newspaper of that name. Murphy was to get his first taste of opposition tactics which were more to do with intimidation than rugby ability. 'They had a forward called Fisher who was older than me and a great deal bigger. He was about fifteen stone. He picked me up early in the game and warned me what he would do with me if I tried to be clever, before dropping me like a rag doll on the floor. I made sure he never got hold of me again in that match. We licked them easily. I scored four tries.' Murphy's dashing display earned him applause from his team-mates and the opposition, and Harry Cook took note.

St Austin's School eventually succumbed in the area final to a powerful side from All Saints, Wigan. The Wigan team included seven lads who eventually went on to turn professional including the great half-back David Bolton, later to tour Australia and New Zealand with Murphy in Great Britain's colours and to become an outstanding player with Wigan.

Inevitably, Murphy forced himself on to the attentions of the Lancashire county schoolboy selectors when he was only fourteen but the experience of his first selection failed to spark his enthusiasm. Though outwardly pleased that the committee was taking notice of him, he was inwardly angry at being named only as a reserve for a county trial at Wigan's Central Park.

A week before the trial Murphy was selected for the St Helens Town team against their great rivals Widnes. He realized it would be a unique opportunity for him to make the Lancashire selectors think again. In the Widnes match the scrum-half opposing Murphy was the Lancashire no. 7 – Ian Hatton. In the Saints dressing-room before the game Murphy had one self-motivating thought: to outshine Hatton and show the doubters on the Lancashire selection committee that he was the best schoolboy half-back in the county.

The Saints chairman, Harry Cook, waited eagerly for the contest, already convinced that Murphy had no equal on the rugby field at this level. Indeed, Widnes had no answer to the fired-up Murphy, who ran in four tries with a performance that catapulted him into the county trial team the following week and left people in no doubt that a very special talent had arrived. In the St Helens boardroom Harry Cook could barely wait for the arrival of Murphy's sixteenth birthday and a chance to offer him a professional career at Knowsley Road.

In the county trial Murphy was able to demonstrate his effortless skills and all-round ability, and was promptly named in the team to play Yorkshire at Knowsley Road. This would be his first big representative match and he knew that his career was underway. Neil Fox, another great half-back, later to tour Australia and New Zealand with Murphy, was in the

Yorkshire team. 'Neil was a hard lad and a magnificent player. But we were too good for them on the day and won comfortably,' Murphy recalls. The 24–16 winning margin indicated the tough job Lancashire had had in gaining the ascendency, but it was the Lancashire half-back pairing that was to be talked about for weeks following the game. Murphy played at scrum-half with Jackie Edwards at stand-off. It was an explosive partnership reckoned by many good judges to be the best half-back pairing in the country at schoolboy level. A crowd of over 18,000 turned up to watch, confirming the drawing power of Murphy's growing reputation. Murphy and Edwards, whose son Shaun has proved himself an outstanding utility back for Wigan and Great Britain and who was appointed club captain in 1988, displayed almost telepathic understanding as Yorkshire were overwhelmed.

The two youngsters became close friends. But Murphy was devastated when Jackie Edwards subsequently signed professional forms for Warrington. 'It was a real disappointment to me when Jackie signed for Warrington. He'd promised me we would stick together as a pair and I believed him. I was really upset when we split up.'

In his early teens Murphy was always keen to play rugby whenever the chance offered itself. He was happiest with a ball in his hands whether it was for his school team, the town or county teams or just a friendly game with friends in the local park. On Sunday afternoons, after the pubs had closed, the older men used to challenge the younger ones to a game on the local field. The married men would play against the single men for a side-stake of a shilling a head with the first team to thirty points to be declared the winner.

Murphy couldn't resist the chance to make extra pocket money but his brother Billy discouraged him from playing because he felt his younger brother was too small and could get hurt. Murphy told his brother bluntly that he was a better player than him and appealed to his father for a second opinion. His father, always keen to encourage Murphy's rugby, agreed and loaned him the shilling side-stake to take part.

The single men were glad to have someone of Murphy's talent playing for them and he became a regular on the wing 'to keep him out of harm's way.' It proved a profitable time for Murphy and his team. 'I had freedom on the wing and my pace was too much for the older men. I regularly scored tries,' he recalls.

But the danger of such undisciplined games was soon to be seen. Murphy and his friends had dug a trench on the field used for the Sunday afternoon challenge matches but had forgotten to mention it to anyone. The local schoolboys used the trench as a den and covered it with sticks and grass to camouflage it from other kids in the neighbourhood. 'One Sunday afternoon we were playing and the married men got the ball. My brother-in-law, Teddy, went hurtling down the field for what looked a certain try when he suddenly disappeared in a flurry of grass, sods and sticks. He had fallen into our den. We pulled him out and the other married men moaned about him not scoring a try. Then we all realized that he was really hurt; indeed, it was discovered that he had broken his leg.'

During another Sunday afternoon game the ambulance was called again to the field to take an injured player to hospital. Bernard Murphy — no relation to Alex — was playing for the single men's team alongside Murphy when catastrophe struck.

'Bernard could run although he couldn't play. The married men's team were tiring and Bernard received the ball on the wing and hurtled towards the try-line. We needed the try to clinch the match and win a shilling each. Unfortunately Bernard kept his head down and ran straight into a prickly bush. We pulled him out with a crown of thorns and with lines of blood running down his face. He had to be taken to hospital for a blood transfusion. He was in a bad way but at the time we had little sympathy because he hadn't grounded the ball for a try.'

Meanwhile, Murphy's appearance as an outstanding schoolboy for the St Austin's and Town teams had brought him to the attention of the legendary Jim Sullivan, the St Helens coach. An established Rugby Union star with Cardiff while still a teenager, Sullivan turned professional with Wigan in 1921 for a then record fee. His goal-kicking feats from full-back re-wrote the record books, starting with more than 100 points in his first season at Central Park. He was captain of the first Wembley Cup-winning team when the event moved to the Empire Stadium in 1929. Wigan beat Dewsbury 13–2 and Sullivan's third-minute goal brought the first points to be recorded in a Rugby League final at Wembley. Sullivan went on to become an outstanding coach, taking Wigan and then St Helens to no less than six Wembley finals, winning four of them, still a record achievement. Such was the quality and pedigree of the man Murphy grew to love and respect: 'He was like a second father to me,' Murphy says.

Jim Sullivan knew all about Murphy's reputation when the fifteen-year-old was invited to the St Helens summer training school. Neither Sullivan nor Harry Cook expressed any interest in Murphy when he left St Austin's despite his efforts to impress them during the summer.

Murphy was downhearted, not realizing that St Helens were perfectly well aware of the size of the talent in front of them. The two men were waiting for the right moment to pounce because they realized that undue interest from them then would alert other clubs, and until he was sixteen no one could sign Murphy.

An invitation to train with the St Helens professional squad at the start of the 1954–55 season raised his hopes. However, he was to get his first lesson from the master. Sullivan asked him how fast he could run, knowing the youngster was very quick off the mark. Murphy's reply left him in no doubt: 'I'm faster than anything you have here,' he boasted. Sullivan had expected that sort of reply. He asked three of his fastest players to line up with Murphy for a race down the St Helens track. Frank Carlton, Eric Ledger and Alec Davies, all even-time men over a hundred yards, lined up alongside Murphy, only to leave him gasping for breath and trailing by twenty yards as they pulled up at the end of the sprint.

Murphy's loss of pride was too much to endure and he went straight to coach Sullivan: 'I'm not coming back here again,' he said. Sullivan put a consoling arm around his shoulders and told him: 'Come back every Tuesday and Thursday for training and we'll see what happens.' Twelve months later Murphy ran against the same three men and beat them easily. The master's first lesson was over.

Murphy was still playing for St Austin's 'old boys' intermediate team in the fifteen-to-seventeen age-group, and his weekly training sessions with St Helens gave him such an edge that he was frequently named player-of-the-match. Early in 1955, as the season was reaching its final stages, Jim Sullivan's team was having an indifferent time. Injuries to key players hadn't helped and international duty had meant that they were without their Great Britain tourists, Dougie Greenall and Alan Prescott, for several matches.

There was going to be little joy or honours for Saints, but Harry Cook and Sullivan had their sights focused on the Junior Cup final to be staged at Knowsley Road on Thursday 21 April 1955 – the eve of Murphy's sixteenth birthday. It was to be the culmination of an exhausting period for the young Murphy who only days before the cup final had also played in tough matches for the town and county schoolboy teams. But he couldn't wait to skipper St Austin's in the final against a strong Rivington Institute side for the Supporters Cup. He knew Jim Sullivan would be watching, and he knew the St Helens directors would be there. He needed no more motivation to do well. With an impressive performance, he believed a call might come to join Saints, though the most he hoped for was to be asked to train again with the players the following season.

Playing in front of a big crowd in the Junior Cup final didn't worry him. As a schoolboy he'd been used to crowds of over 8,000 at Brown Edge, where St Austin's played their home matches. He was bothered more about his chances of playing for St Helens. No one from the club had made a move, though he knew they were interested. With such thoughts going through his mind Murphy led his team out for the final with one purpose – to show the powers that be at St Helens that he was too good a catch to miss.

Another big crowd was present and Murphy didn't disappoint them. In a performance of power and pace the young St Austin's skipper dominated the game with a hat-trick of tries and an all-round display of his full repertoire of skills. A bewildered Rivington team were overwhelmed 41–8 and the Knowsley Road crowd roared their approval as Murphy held the cup high.

Within hours his professional career with St Helens was to begin, though Murphy himself still had pangs of doubt as he left the field to a standing ovation. After a quick bath, Murphy dressed for an evening out with his team-mates to celebrate their win. As he waited for the other lads to change he wondered about his future. He had still had no firm inquiry from St Helens and he had no professional qualifications to help him to a career.

But events were moving fast, literally over his head. Immediately above the dressing-rooms at Knowsley Road is the club's boardroom. Murphy was asked to report there to the chairman, who wanted to speak to him. In the boardroom were Harry Cook and a group of serious-looking men including his father, James, Jim Sullivan and two directors, Lionel Swift and Joe Harrison. Murphy didn't know it, but a cloak and dagger operation had already been planned to occupy the hours until midnight when he would be old enough to sign professional forms. Afterwards Murphy was to realize that Jim Sullivan's part in the kidnapping operation was designed to keep other interested clubs away from him in the hours between the end of the Junior Cup final and midnight – his sixteenth birthday.

'Sully took me down the back stairs so nobody would see us,' says Murphy. 'And when I signed after midnight he was laughing and admitted that he knew nine other clubs had wanted my signature.' Sullivan also told Murphy's father on the night of the signing: 'We've got ourselves a diamond.' Harry Cook recalls the evening with a smile: 'Alex's parents knew we were going to sign him on the stroke of midnight. But we had to watch the opposition all the time. We had no hold on any of these boys.'

Murphy was smuggled out of the club down the back stairs,

and into a car which sped away to Harry Cook's home, a few miles from the St Helens ground. There he was given orange juice and biscuits and a pep talk as the hours ticked away to midnight. As the evening wore on Murphy became increasingly irritable. He told his captors he'd had enough of waiting around. 'I just wanted to go home to my mother. I was used to being in bed early and I was very tired.'

However Murphy's signature was still not on the forms which would make him a St Helens player so it was decided to make another move to keep him interested and awake as the hours dragged on to midnight. Director Joe Harrison's house had a snooker table – just the thing to occupy the youngster. So the group headed for Harrison's home in Millbrook Lane. Mrs Iris Hunter, whose husband Harold was a prominent member of the St Helens board, lived near the Harrisons. She recalls the evening in detail: 'They came across to our house for beer to keep the men going. We knew how keen they were to sign Alex. All the big clubs were after him. I remember Warrington, Wigan, Leeds all wanted him.'

Mrs Hunter and her husband had followed Murphy's career from his early schooldays. 'We liked him and looked after him. He was always impressive even as a little boy. I remember him scoring a try in a junior match once, and before anybody could move he'd picked up the ball and kicked the goal himself. That's how confident he was in his ability even as a little boy. Alex was a born player but a rum sod as well. But you put up with a lot if you have a genius. And where rugby was concerned Alex was a genius.'

2
Saint Alex

So it was that shortly after midnight on 22 April 1955 – the opening minutes of Murphy's sixteenth birthday – a very tired teenager, watched by Harry Cook, two Saints directors, Messrs Swift and Harrison, Murphy's father, James, and the club coach, Jim Sullivan, signed professional forms for St Helens. He was rewarded with the princely sum of £80 but the money didn't matter. Murphy had realized his boyhood dream. He'd become a 'Saint'.

Murphy knew that other clubs had been prepared to pay upwards of £1,500 for his signature, but he decided from the start that there was only one club for him and that was St Helens. Harry Cook advised him to look after his career outside rugby. He also told the sleepy youngster that if he wanted to give the money to anyone then he should give it to his parents. 'They have looked after you and brought you up,' was his fatherly advise. The Saints chairman always reminded boys who signed professional forms that rugby was a hard game and if possible they should put the money away. 'I used to tell them if they wanted to look after anyone at all it should be their mums and dads. Alex was a very cocky lad,' Cook

15

remembers, 'but he was also a belting scrum-half, there's no doubt about it. He was always polite and a really smashing lad to deal with. He just wanted to play for St Helens. The incentive too often with sportsmen is money but not in those days and not with Murphy. All the boys had just one ambition – to play for their own town team.'

Murphy was soon to endear himself to the wife of his hero and coach Jim Sullivan. Mrs Eve Sullivan remembers the words of her husband after Murphy had signed professional forms: 'He told me, "This lad will be a belter. He has everything." And he had. A wonderful sense of timing and safe hands. I remember his sense of anticipation was uncanny. He could think a move ahead of other players and had perfect ball-handling and control. I watched some of the world's finest footballers during my husband's distinguished career but you could tell straightaway that Alex was going to be something special.'

'Mrs Jim', as Eve Sullivan was affectionately known to her friends and the players, also recognized there was another side to the young Murphy. 'There are no two ways about it; he was a little sod at times. Jim and I were like a second father and mother to him. But he wasn't always a saint; you take it from me. And he could be a dirty player. If he could get away with anything, he would try. But when he played, something different always happened on the pitch. He had such power in his legs and such ability to make things happen. Of course, people disliked him because he talked too much. He was always opening his mouth and telling people what he thought. But those who disliked him for that didn't really understand him. If you knew him well he was always a likable and generous man.'

After signing for St Helens, Murphy took his father's and Harry Cook's advice to get himself a back-up career outside rugby. He trained as a miner and went to a pit a few miles from home, hoping to be transferred eventually to the Leigh Green colliery, which was nearer to St Helens. He got out of bed at 14.30 each morning to catch a bus to work, arriving home late in the evening, drained of energy and tired. When the work began to affect his training sessions with St Helens, and the promise of a transfer didn't materialize, on his father's orders he gave up the job. A promise to transfer him then was too late and the young Murphy promptly found himself another career outlet as an apprentice joiner with St Helens Corporation.

There Murphy was to meet and become firm friends with the St Helens 'A' team coach, Bill Mercer. He was by now completely absorbed in his rugby and in the mid-week evening training sessions under Jim Sullivan, and eagerly awaited the start of his first professional season – 1955–56.

In August, the young Alex Murphy made his professional bow in the St Helens 'A' team at Knowsley Road. An outstanding display, with dazzling 45-yard solo try under the Widnes posts, helped his team to a comfortable win and Murphy left the field to sustained applause just as he had done in the Junior Cup final some months earlier on the eve of his signing. From that moment he was established as a favourite with the St Helens supporters though Jim Sullivan realized that he must keep the feet of his star pupil firmly on the ground.

News of the young Murphy's prowess on the field was spreading. After another faultless display and two superb tries in the defeat of Liverpool 'A', followed by a breathtaking 75-yard solo try in the crushing defeat of Blackpool 'A' at Knowsley Road, he was being described already as a future international.

In the hard game of Rugby League, however, it was only a matter of time before an opposing side would try to bring the young upstart from St Helens down to earth. Murphy was about to be given a hard lesson in a match against Wigan reserves. It was one of the few games watched by his mother, and she shudders at the memory. Murphy, running riot, had scored a spectacular 40-yard try, his speed leaving the Wigan defence in turmoil. But as he tried to make a run on the blind side of the scrum, certain that his extra pace would take him clear of any trouble he was suddenly flattened by a Wigan forward who had anticipated the move. He left the field in the arms of his trainer, semi-conscious with blood pouring from a head wound.

His mother watched in horror: 'I remember someone in the crowd shouted, "Leave him there, we'll come back tomorrow and bury him." It was cruel to hear. I told his father later: "If that's your Rugby League you can keep it."'

The incident confirmed Mrs Murphy's worst fears about the chosen career of her youngest child. 'I had worked for the Pilkington glass people for twenty-seven years and hoped to give him a better start in life. I was terrified of him getting hurt. I didn't like the idea of him getting knocked down so much. I tried to stop him but he wouldn't listen. He was always a strong-willed boy and spoke his mind. But Rugby League's a very hard game, and I used to wonder sometimes if it would deprive me of a son.'

On the 1958 Great Britain tour to Australia and New Zealand, Vinty Karalius, another great St Helens player and the loose forward who protected Murphy on the field, wrote to Mrs Murphy to say that her Alex had been hurt. 'I got a sinking feeling in my stomach. I wrote back warning Vinty that if anything happened to Alex he was not to mention a rugby ball to me again.'

Murphy was learning the professional game fast and felt he should be given an early chance in the first team after several outstanding performances in the reserves. In those days at St Helens the board of directors, after consultation with the coach, picked the team. Chairman Cook recalls Murphy's impatience and that of his father: 'His dad used constantly to ask me when I was going to play his son in the first team. But I felt Alex was too young and his bones and muscles were not properly set. After all he was only sixteen.' However, circumstances were to force the hand of the directors and led to Murphy getting his first-team call-up.

St Helens had hit form in the early rounds of the Challenge Cup and when they overcame the holders, Barrow, in the semi-final, after a replay, Wembley euphoria hit the town. There were several matches to be played before Wembley and the directors decided that they had to utilize the whole playing strength or risk serious injury to key players before the final. So Murphy, still only sixteen, was named for his first-team debut in a night match against Whitehaven at Knowsley Road. And he wasn't the only youngster in the team. Skipper for the night was George Parsons, the only player with first-team experience.

It was the opportunity Murphy had been waiting for. He responded with a display showing his full range of skills, scoring a superb try with a burst of pace that left the opposition full-back stranded, and making others for his team-mates. St Helens won 22–7 and Harry Cook knew that it would be difficult to protect Murphy from the toughness of first-team duty after such a display. It was Murphy's first senior bonus, a winning pay packet he felt he'd more than earned, and he waited for congratulations from the great Jim Sullivan. He was in for a surprise. Instead of a slap on the back from the great man he was given a roasting for the things he had done wrong during the game. Sullivan listed his faults and ordered him to do extra training the same evening. Murphy, thoroughly deflated, was close to tears.

The season ended with St Helens beating Halifax 13–2 in the Wembley final to win the Challenge Cup. Murphy saw the effect it had had on the club, its supporters and the town of St Helens and privately vowed to make himself a regular in the first team the following season and to show Jim Sullivan just what he was made of. For Sullivan that Wembley final was his greatest triumph at St Helens since he'd joined the club from Wigan four years earlier, and made up for the bitter disappointment of the Wembley defeat by Huddersfield in 1953.

John 'Todder' Dickinson, who had missed the final against Halifax through injury, and Austin Rhodes, another outstanding product of Murphy's St Austin's School, were the reigning half-back pairing at St Helens and Murphy set his sights on breaking it up. In October 1956, a few weeks into Murphy's second season as a professional, he was named in the first team again for the visit of Workington. Though at first simply in the squad, Murphy replaced Rhodes during the game, scored a try and was promptly dropped. He was bewildered and angry at being treated so badly, and told his father so.

Two first-team appearances against Whitehaven and Workington in twenty months at the club wasn't the career progress that the impatient Murphy had envisaged. It was time to take action, he believed, and to insist on knowing why he was being constantly overlooked. He went with his father to confront Harry Cook and the St Helens board, though it was denied at the time that he'd asked for a transfer. Anyway, the chairman realized that it was pointless to try to hold back such talent any longer: 'His ability forced the issue. He trained hard, looked after himself and his natural ability did the rest.'

Murphy decided that the best way to back his father's justifiable demands was to stake his claim for a regular first-team place by proving he was too good to be left out. In the coming weeks he did just that. The Knowsley Road crowd gave him a standing ovation after a superb solo try as the Saints 'A' team conquered Leigh, and he followed that with an even better performance against Oldham 'A', grabbing two tries in an outstanding display. Now the fans were backing his father in his demands that the young Murphy should be given an extended run in the first team.

Meanwhile, the 'Bring back Murphy' campaign on the terraces was being overshadowed by reports that St Helens were again pursuing the legendary Welsh Rugby Union stand-off, Cliff Morgan. A big signing-on fee was thought to be the bait. However, the rumours quickly faded away and Murphy was back in the headlines and on the lips of the fans. More speculation followed that Murphy was so fed up he was about to demand a transfer and then ended with his recall against Warrington in January 1957. He responded in typical fashion. Another spectacular try in a 33–7 St Helens victory was the signal for Murphy to show his consistency with a try a game in his first five games after being recalled to the first team.

At Easter, St Helens ended a fruitless 1956–57 season despite scoring over 1,000 points. It was Sullivan's poorest season since taking over five years earlier and Murphy, now a first-team regular though only seventeen, felt a keen sense of anti-climax. He played in the closing three games, crammed into four days, and ending with a match against Blackpool Borough at Knowsley Road. Murphy brought the curtain down with a thrilling performance which underlined his flourishing talent as St Helens trounced Blackpool 48–10. It was the day of Murphy's eighteenth birthday. Within months he was to explode on to the world stage.

During the summer Murphy continued to train alone, determined not to lose his sharpness. He ticked off the days to the opening match in August, a pre-season curtain-raiser against Barrow. The big charity-match crowd roared their approval of Murphy's every touch as he orchestrated play throughout the afternoon. Murphy was determined to start the season on the right note and stormed in for a hat-trick in the 79–13 annihilation of Barrow which left their more experienced players shaking their heads in admiring disbelief at his audacity and skill. Murphy's absolute determination to establish himself in the no. 7 jersey had been announced and he went on to score thirty tries that season. Jim Sullivan told his wife Eve on the evening of the Barrow match: 'This lad has everything. He's going to be famous.'

His words were more prophetic than even the great Sullivan could have imagined at the time: within months Murphy was to become Britain's youngest-ever tourist to Australia and New Zealand.

In the first league match, following his impressive game against Barrow, Murphy was on the try-scorers' list again as St Helens won at Widnes. The international selectors were being urged in the press to take a closer look at the youngster with the truly outstanding talent. Harry Cook smiled knowingly. In his weekly talks with Jim Sullivan, when they discussed the club's playing strength, Alex Murphy's name dominated their conversations. Even Sullivan, a playing and now a coaching legend in his own right, was astounded by Murphy's all-round ability. Moreover, 'Alex was a dream to handle,' says Harry Cook, recalling those days. 'He was eager and dedicated in his training: he was always first out and last in, I remember. Rugby was his life and he gave it one hundred and one per cent effort.'

Meanwhile dramatic events were taking shape thousands of miles away in South Africa which were to have an explosive impact on Murphy's burgeoning career and undoubtedly helped to guarantee him a place on the world stage. The Saints chairman was playing a game of poker yet again but this time for very high stakes indeed, and he was to outmanoeuvre everyone to scoop the kitty. The 'kitty' this time was South Africa's great Rugby Union winger, Karel Thomas Van Vollenhoven. Cook believed that, with Vollenhoven on the wing outside him, Murphy would be unstoppable.

A cloak of secrecy was thrown around the negotiations as St Helens went about the business of luring the magnificent Springbok to Knowsley Road. At the eleventh hour Cook thought his weeks of closely guarded talks and planning were about to prove fruitless. Vollenhoven was interesting other clubs and there were strong rumours linking him with other teams.

Warrington had shown interest in Vollenhoven after he'd been chosen for the South African summer tour of Australia in 1956. There the Springbok had watched his first Rugby League match and realized that the League code offered tremendous scope for wingers. But Warrington's interest was now lukewarm and it was Wigan who decided to move in with a cash bid. Vollenhoven was promised £2,000 for his signature and Harry Cook and his contacts abroad realized they must act quickly if they were to succeed. It was touch and go.

'I thought we had lost him,' admits Cook. 'I made two telephone calls to South Africa and Tom indicated he might be talking to someone else. I said to him, "Tom, you've given your word to come to St Helens." He paused, and then said, "Okay." I was a very relieved man to hear that,' Cook recalls. So for the price of two long-distance phone calls the legendary Vollenhoven gave his word to St Helens, and an athlete of consummate ability had become a 'Saint'. Vollenhoven's pedigree was awesome: he had run the 100 yards in 9·8 seconds when running against Germany for Northern Transvaal; and had recorded a long jump of 24 feet 5 inches. Now Harry Cook could hardly wait for him to put on a Saints jersey alongside Murphy. He knew the fans were in for a rare treat.

Murphy's first reaction to the arrival of the South African

superstar was one of indifference. When Jim Sullivan asked Murphy to teach Vollenhoven how to pass the ball he replied: 'If he's that good he can teach himself.' But he soon warmed to the brilliance of the flying Springbok and they became firm friends.

Vollenhoven arrived in St Helens in a glare of publicity during October 1957, about the time that Harry Cook announced a revolutionary change in club policy. In future Jim Sullivan was to have full control over first-team selection. Of course, Vollenhoven was into the side, and on Saturday 26 October 1957, 'the Van' as he became known to Saints supporters, made his much-heralded debut in front of a packed Knowsley Road.

Many experts believe it was that day that started Murphy on his outstanding international career. Leeds provided powerful opposition for Vollenhoven's debut but though eyes were on 'the Van' it was Murphy at scrum-half who turned in a brilliant performance, hailed as 'international class' by the press. Even for the superb Vollenhoven, Murphy was reluctant to relinquish the spotlight. Producing bursts of speed and power which left the Leeds cover defence gasping, Murphy ripped Leeds apart with three stunning tries and was involved in the move which led to Vollenhoven's 45-yard debut try in the closing minutes to clinch a 36–7 victory. Murphy and Vollenhoven were clapped from the field. A week later Saints won at Whitehaven 15–7 to go top of the league: 'the Van' scored another superb try but it was Murphy with a lightning burst of speed and touch-down who clinched the victory.

Within weeks another full house at Knowsley Road looked on spellbound as Swinton were swept aside 43–11. They just couldn't hold the combined power and pace of Murphy and Vollenhoven as each flew in for a hat-trick of tries. Cook's prophecy about the effect of the Murphy-Vollenhoven pairing was coming true. Crowds were flocking to watch the two great players, and the international selectors had already pencilled Murphy's name into a possible tour place.

When the teams for the first tour trial were announced in March 1958, Murphy's name was included. Frustratingly, a snow-storm forced the abandonment of that trial but Murphy was promptly named for the second trial, at Leeds, the following week for the Rest against a Great Britain team. Wearing the no. 7 jersey for the Great Britain side was the experienced John Fishwick, of Rochdale Hornets, later to become one of Murphy's back-room boys at St Helens. 'Fishwick was a good 'un and had a very good trial game,' concedes Murphy, 'I thought I'd blown it.'

However, unknown to Murphy, his St Helens skipper, Alan Prescott, was pushing Murphy's claims for a tour place and Brian Pitchford, his future boss at Warrington, believed that Murphy had already done enough to book his tour place. "Murph" was full of himself. He'd played superbly in the trial game. I remember that after the match he put his arm around the league secretary, Bill Fallowfield, in the dressing-room and said to him, "Okay, who are the other twenty-five who will be going on tour with me?" He knew then, even as a teenager, how good he was.'

The following Monday morning Murphy was awakened by his father at 6 o'clock. Murphy senior was holding a letter telling him that Alex had been selected as Great Britain's youngest-ever tourist. 'Normally my dad had to ask me twice to get out of bed. That morning I leapt out and ran down the stairs to make sure the letter was real. It was a morning I shall never forget.'

Murphy was one of six Saints players who eventually made the tour, along with skipper Alan Prescott, Glyn Moses, Frank Carlton, Vinty Karalius, and Abe Terry. After his selection, St Helens had a disappointing end to the season, losing by a single point to Workington, 13–14, in the championship play-offs although Murphy almost saved the day for Saints with three superb drop-goals. This was a ploy which had now become his forte and which he perfected to such an extent that he eventually forced the league to reduce the points value of drop-goals to one point.

Murphy was on tenterhooks waiting for the tour party to leave England, and then they had to endure agonizing delays on the 12,000-mile journey to Australia. The tourists left on the first leg of the journey, bound for Zurich, on 12 May 1958. Then the plane was turned back because of engine-trouble. When they eventually arrived at Zurich there was a second delay as the plane taking them on to Beirut developed a mechanical fault. Murphy was terrified: 'I had only seen butterflies in the air before. It was the first time I'd flown and I was beginning to get butterflies myself,' he says.

The stranded tourists stayed in Zurich overnight to await a replacement aircraft and eventually they were on their way again. But a Murphy prank nearly misfired. While waiting in the airport lounge in Zurich to board their flight to Beirut, Murphy picked up a cigarette lighter which he thought one of the lads had left behind. 'As we were going through customs I realized that I might be charged duty on the lighter, so I slipped it into Abe Terry's coat pocket. He was nearly locked up for not declaring it, despite his protests that he didn't know it was in his pocket. He'd have killed me if I'd owned up. So I kept quiet.'

The tourists arrived in Sydney two days late and only twenty-four hours before their opening game. The Olympic Hotel, near the Cricket Ground, where the party was staying, 'was like a western saloon', Murphy recalls. 'It was ideal for a tour party. If you did any damage it wouldn't be noticed because it wouldn't have looked any different. The landlady was magnificent. A superb Australian woman who looked after us like our own mothers. She was brilliant. The Aussies are the best people in the world to entertain you and look after you, but very hard to play against because they want to win.'

Murphy recalls the day the players were invited to a race-meeting. He was introduced to Keith Holman, the great Aussie scrum-half, who would be opposing him during the Test series. 'Meet the best scrum-half in the world,' said the man introducing them. Quick as his playing style, Murphy countered, 'It's very nice of you to say that about me before Keith has even played against us.'

Despite the agony of the delays on the journey from England, Great Britain won all their opening games except for a 24–24 draw with a tough Western Districts side. It was in that game that Murphy gave notice of his ability, scoring a magnificent long-range solo try after selling two dummies. The Australian press was quick to point out his threat.

After such an impressive start to the tour, Great Britain were hot favourites for the first Test on Saturday 14 June 1958, at the Sydney Cricket Ground. It was Murphy's international debut and he was full of himself. His confidence took a hammering, however, as the tourists were thrashed 25–8 in front of 80,000 excited Australians, and Murphy's in-experience was exposed to the full. 'Every time Keith Holman got the ball he told me he was going to kick me all the way to Sydney. Instead of trying to use my pace I tried to run through him. I was taught a lesson I shall never forget. I went back to my hotel room and cried.'

Great Britain's captain, Alan Prescott, Murphy's team-mate at St Helens, had no sympathy for him and blasted him for playing the wrong kind of game on his Test debut. 'He told me to use my pace if I was ever picked again on the tour. He said he doubted whether I would get back in but if I did I must use my pace to full advantage or he would want to know why.' Murphy never looked back after that Prescott lecture. The 'baby' of the tour party had grown up overnight and was to become the key figure in Great Britain's Ashes-winning series.

Two days after the first Test defeat Murphy produced a match-winning performance as the tourists bounced back, beating a strong Brisbane side 34–29. Tries on either side of half-time from Murphy again stamped him as the game's outstanding player, and his Great Britain team-mates clapped the teenager off at the end of the game. The Australian press was generous in their praise of Murphy's brilliance at scrum-half in the next game, which brought them another convincing win over a strong Queensland side. Confidence was now fully restored and Australian pride was about to be dealt a severe blow.

Off-the-field problems, however, threatened to disrupt the tourists' plans. The coach, Jim Brough, angered the players by imposing an early evening curfew. Anger at losing the first Test was still felt and matters weren't helped when a prank turned sour. Bennett Manson, one of two tour managers with Tom Mitchell, ordered Dick Huddart to catch the next plane home as a disciplinary measure. Murphy recalls the incident: 'Dick threw a firework into a telephone-box while Manson was phoning England. Manson was furious and ordered him home. The lads held a meeting and decided that if Huddart was ordered back to England we would all go home with him.' The drama was kept from the press but the tour was nearly wrecked as the players locked horns with the tour management.

However, as the temperature cooled down, Tom Mitchell enjoyed a bigger say in day-to-day affairs. Murphy admired Mitchell: 'Tom Mitchell had a white beard and used always to carry a book. He looked like a prophet. But he was brilliant. Tom always left his room light on so that we knew he was there. It was only on the last night of the tour that we found out he was never in his room. The light was left on to kid us and keep us indoors,' laughs Murphy.

Murphy was the live wire of the tour party and was always willing to enjoy a joke. As tension mounted before the second Test, he accepted a bet to climb a nearby hill with Tom Mitchell who was an experienced climber. The pair backed themselves to climb the hill in an hour. 'From the ground it didn't seem all that high but I was terrified when we got near the top, and wanted to turn back,' says Murphy. 'Tom Mitchell mentioned that there were nasty local snakes around. I was at the top and back down within fifteen minutes. Tom was a shrewd man.'

On another occasion the players were relaxing in the hot afternoon sun by swimming in the sea. Murphy had heard stories about fierce man-eating sharks and declined to cool off in the sea. He watched his team-mates splashing about and started chatting to an old man. 'He had a foot missing and part of his arm. He told me he'd been attacked by a shark while swimming in the same spot as the lads were using. I shouted to them and pointed to the old man. At the word "shark" they came out of the water quicker than you could blink.'

Such incidents helped to ease tension and sustain morale

before the vital second Test in Brisbane on Saturday 5 July. Great Britain had to win to keep the series alive but the game started disastrously for the tourists. Within minutes, the skipper, Alan Prescott, couldn't use his right arm, which was subsequently found to be broken. After a quarter of an hour, the stand-off, David Bolton, was on his way to hospital with a broken collar-bone. Jim Challinor, Eric Fraser and Vinty Karalius were also hurt in this battle for Ashes survival.

At half-time Great Britain, despite their problems, were leading 10–2 on a bucketful of guts and courage. Alan Prescott, despite medical advice, decided the team couldn't do without him and again took the field. It was a courageous decision which fired the dressing-room. Karalius moved from loose forward to stand-off for the injured Bolton, and with the Australian crowd jeering, the stage was set for Murphy to produce his own special brand of brilliance. Within minutes the crowd were on their feet, cheering reluctantly at the brilliance of Murphy who was now orchestrating play.

Murphy laid on three tries as Great Britain pulled away from Australia to square the series with a courageous 25–18 victory. The try that left the packed house gasping was one he scored himself from 75 yards out. Breaking from the scrum, he accelerated away from two tackles, drew the remnants of the Australian cover defence, and threw a long pass to Karalius straining to stay in support. Karalius held off two Australian defenders before flipping the ball back one-handed to Murphy now going at full speed and unstoppable as he rocketed to the line between the Australian posts. Murphy recalls the moment: 'Vinty shouted to me to head for the corner before running round the back of the posts. He reckoned I'd get my head stuck if I went between the posts.' Murphy's man-of-the-match performance and Prescott's courage had levelled the series when all seemed lost.

The crucial third Test to decide the Ashes was to be played at the Sydney Cricket Ground on 19 July. Before the match, the tourists stayed at the seaside resort of Cronulla, overlooking the Pacific breakers, while Murphy prepared to put the seal on his reputation with another performance which had even the Australians in ecstasy throughout.

Australia had lost not only the crucial psychological battle but also the forward battle, largely due to Murphy's brilliance and the fearsome tackling of Vinty Karalius, now to be known as the 'wild bull of the pampas'.

The day of the big game arrived and Great Britain were confident but on edge. They realized what was at stake for themselves and their supporters back home after the *débâcle* of the first Test on the same ground. However, Prescott's bravery in the previous Test, which had levelled the series, was still fresh in the minds of the British team, and was a continuing source of inspiration. Murphy says: 'Prescott was the most courageous captain I have ever played under. Without his bravery and inspiration in the second Test we would certainly have lost the series.'

Sydney Cricket Ground was bursting at the seams on the day of the match and Murphy gave early warning that he was on top of his game with a brilliant burst from the scrum which had the Australian cover at full stretch to pull him down. 'Johnny Raper, the Australian loose forward, had never been passed on the blind side, they had told me before the game. I passed him before he got his head out of the scrum. That immediately gave us the edge.' Murphy flew from the scrum, beat two men with a swerving run, broke clear of a tackle as another Australian half-back tried to haul him down, and went half the length of the field for a sensational try which had the biased Australian crowd on their feet in admiration. 'As I passed the Aussie full-back Gordon Clifford, I gave him his father's best wishes. (Murphy had met Clifford's father a few days before and promised to pass on the message if he saw his son.) When I touched down behind the sticks Clifford chased after me and threatened to kick me into the back of the stand. He obviously had a poor sense of humour.'

The angry crowd of 75,000, yelling for an Australian victory, had reached breaking point as Murphy now controlled the game. They took their frustration out on the referee, Jack Casey, from Queensland, pelting him with bottles and orange peel. The British tourists also came in for a barrage as they left the field after an emphatic victory 40–17, the highest winning margin in Tests between the two countries.

The next day the Australian press was full of praise for Murphy's impact on the Test match and on the series as a whole. Headlines such as 'Brilliant Murphy Wins Game For Tourists', and 'The Little Genius From St Helens', told their own story. Murphy was also described as 'the finest attacking scrum-half' the Australians had ever seen. Murphy remembers the words of the man he admired, Keith Holman, the Australian scrum-half, rated by many to have been the best in the world until Murphy arrived. Holman told him: 'We've lost the match and the series. A new king has arrived.' From that moment the two men became firm friends, bonded by mutual respect in the toughest game in the world.

Clinching the Ashes, of course, called for a celebration in the British camp. Back at the team's hotel everyone was in high spirits and Murphy, who normally drank orange juice, celebrated with his team-mates. 'Glyn Moses, our full-back, had to carry me to bed I felt so tipsy. I was just glad my dad wasn't going to find out.' Meanwhile news of Murphy's Australian feats had been flashed to his home town of St Helens, and the hottest property in the game was attracting rumour and speculation with every try he scored as St Helens officials tried to dampen down reports that Murphy had been offered a king's ransom to settle in Australia.

Murphy's parents were being asked in the street if their son was coming back home or staying in Australia. When Murphy did arrive back in Thatto Heath to a hero's welcome, his mother was taken aback. She told his father: 'Jimmy, he went out a boy and he's come back a man.' She also felt a massive sense of relief that her youngest was back in one piece. 'I didn't want him to be a Rugby League player in the first place. I was terrified of him getting hurt. I remember the morning his father told me he'd been picked for the tour. My heart sank. I didn't want anything to happen to him and here he was still a teenager and picked to go to Australia. I could have cried.'

The tour had made Murphy an even more complete player and he picked up where he'd left off for St Helens when the new season began, with a man-of-the-match performance in a Lancashire Cup second-round victory over Leigh. More honours were to come his way. In the next game he became the club's youngest ever first-team captain and celebrated with a stunning performance in a 15–8 victory over Wakefield Trinity at Knowsley Road. And he was still only nineteen.

Early the next year, in 1959, the international selectors met to pick the side to meet the French at Headingley on 14 March. Predictably Murphy was named as scrum-half and responded with a dazzling performance which re-wrote the record books. He stormed over the French line four times – a try-scoring feat which still stands as an individual record in the Tests between the countries. Not yet twenty and an established international, the future for Murphy, his country and his beloved St Helens seemed secure.

St Helens had lost in the quarter-finals of the Challenge Cup at Featherstone and there was press speculation about Murphy moving from the scrum-half position to stand-off. Though Murphy didn't entirely agree with the switch he agreed to move for the sake of the team. Though unhappy without the no. 7 on his back, he accepted the situation and concentrated on the forthcoming Championship final against Hunslet at Odsal Stadium, Bradford on 16 May 1959. Over 50,000 fans saw the dynamic Murphy-Vollenhoven partnership crush the Yorkshiremen, with Saints coming from behind to win 44–22. Murphy, the young Saints captain, had sparked the revival with a dazzling move which set up a 75-yard try for Vollenhoven. Murphy, St Helens and their supporters were at the top of the Rugby League tree and the tour 'veteran' was just twenty.

Vollenhoven had scored no less than sixty-two tries in that 1958–59 season – easily the league's top try-scorer. Indeed, he was top try-scorer again the following season, with fifty-four, and ran in another sixty in 1960–61 to complete his hat-trick. To underline the power of St Helens play at that time Murphy was also among the league's top ten try-scorers.

Following his record four-try performance against the French at Leeds in March 1959, Murphy, by now the automatic choice for Great Britain at scrum-half, was in the team for the return in Grenoble a few days before his twentieth birthday. It was his sixteenth international cap. Another came later in the year against Australia (injury deprived him of others in that three-Test series) and he was looking forward eagerly to the World Cup at the start of the following (1960–61) season, his favourite stage on which he was to turn in a champagne performance.

Between seasons, in the June of 1960, Murphy was married in St Austin's Church, Thatto Heath to Alice, a mathematics teacher at St Alban's Secondary School, St Helens. Alice was and is as knowledgeable about Rugby League as she is about teaching maths, and has been at Alex's side through thick and thin ever since. Their daughter, Ann, is another Rugby League enthusiast and watches St Helens play whenever she can.

The opening World Cup match was at Bradford's Odsal Stadium on 24 September 1960. Great Britain, inspired by a Murphy try, beat New Zealand 23–8 in a match noted for its short tempers, vicious tackling and the mercurial Murphy, who taunted the Kiwis with an arrogant display of his skills.

Britain won their second game against the French 33–7 at Swinton with Murphy and his team-mate from St Helens, Vinty Karalius, in the thick of the action, Karalius eventually getting his marching orders along with the French forward, Barthe. 'There was a lot at stake and national pride was running high,' remembers Murphy. 'We were playing in front of our own fans and felt we could win the World Cup, and it rattled the French.'

Britain completed the three-nation clean sweep at Odsal Stadium, the scene of their victory over New Zealand. This time it was Murphy's old adversary, Australia, who were overcome 10–3 in another tough encounter. The Australians realized that Murphy had lost none of his ability as he dominated the scrums and made a try. It was Murphy's tenth cap.

But his best performance was yet to come in Great Britain's victory over a star-studded Rest of the World team in the closing match of the series, again at Odsal. Britain won 33–27 after a great struggle. It was Murphy, with two devastating tries, who made sure of Britain's supremacy. Murphy's half-back partner throughout the series was Frank Myler, who went on to captain and manage a touring side, and now also chipped in with two tries. He had one word for Murphy's performances during the World Cup: 'brilliant'. It was a description thoroughly endorsed by Murphy's fellow professionals from all three countries who gave him the ultimate accolade by voting him the outstanding player of the series.

3
Part of the Union

The 1960s were to enjoy more of Murphy's brilliance. It was also to be a decade which would see him as both hero and villain. It was to bring him despair and heartache after his bitter row with St Helens and the final break with the club. However, before then there was also to be the glory of two winning Challenge Cup finals with Saints, a second tour of Australia and New Zealand, and Murphy endorsing his rugby genius with outstanding displays for the RAF Rugby Union team.

National Service meant that he could play both the professional and amateur codes. He was to surprise many Union experts who felt he would not be able to learn the 'pass and fall' technique of Union scrum-halves, while the majority believed he would be out of his depth under Union rules. On the other hand, the great Lewis Jones, himself a former Rugby Union international, warned his Union friends that in his opinion Murphy was the best scrum-half or stand-off in the world at either code, and would make a great contribution to the Union game.

Murphy's reputation as the world's best scrum-half hadn't

gone unnoticed with the services, and he was first instructed to report to the army camp at Catterick. However, the RAF had other plans for him, and Murphy suddenly found he'd been 'transferred' to the RAF and was told to report to Cardington instead. From there he went to another RAF camp at Bridgnorth before being posted to RAF Haydock beside the famous race-course just a few miles from his St Helens home. The Army's loss was to be very much a gain for the RAF.

Murphy decided to turn it on for his admiring St Helens fans in his farewell game before reporting for national service. A big crowd had turned out for the match against their old rivals Wigan at Knowsley Road. Two brilliant tries in a performance which earned him a standing ovation saw St Helens safely home with an 11–6 victory. As he waved to his fans at the end of the game Murphy headed for life in the RAF.

Murphy's first weekend pass enabled him to play for St Helens in the Lancashire Cup final against Swinton at Central Park. This was a crucial game, for Saints had failed to lift the cup in three out of the previous four finals. Now, however, Aircraftman Murphy was the inspiration behind a 15–9 Saints victory. Twice he burst round the wrong side of the scrum to send in Vollenhoven and then Rhodes for tries. He was at his mercurial best once again, and was named man-of-the-match.

In December 1960 Aircraftman Murphy scored a vital try in Great Britain's 21–10 victory over France in Bordeaux, but the selectors were chancing their arm by naming him for the return match at St Helens at the end of January. The match clashed with the RAF's game against the Harlequins at Twickenham as they prepared for the inter-services tournament in which they hoped Murphy would prove a vital factor in the RAF winning the Services crown.

Great Britain's selectors were delighted when Murphy was given the 'all clear' to gain his twelfth cap. But there was a string attached. Murphy was told he must earn his release for the international game by playing for the RAF against Leicester just two days before. He smiles as he recalls the deal he struck with his commanding officer: 'Before the Leicester game I'd been below par for the RAF team. But my commanding officer wasn't having any nonsense. He told me straight to my face that if I didn't play better I'd be posted to Gan, in the Indian Ocean. I very quickly found my touch again and played my heart out against Leicester.' The RAF won 11–6 and Murphy, at stand-off, produced a world-class performance which had the Leicester players clapping him at the end. Even when the RAF lost to a strong Royal Navy side 9–3 at Twickenham it was again Murphy who earned the accolades. One press report said the Rugby League man had 'single-handed kept the RAF in the game'. Another headline summed up the game thus: 'RAF hero is a League man.'

Again Murphy was the RAF's outstanding player in their 18–6 win over Cambridge University. From stand-off, Murphy kicked three goals and scored two tries to leave Union devotees gasping in admiration for the Great Britain Rugby League scrum-half. Murphy demonstrated precision touch-kicking, brilliant ball-handling and devastating bursts of speed to leave Cambridge in disarray. And he sealed the performance with a 45-yard solo try selling two dummies in his run for the line to leave the Cambridge cover floundering. Murphy was certainly winning the hearts and minds of doubters with his all-round brilliance in the Union game.

One minute, Murphy would be playing brilliantly for the RAF Union team, the next he would be equally outstanding for St Helens and Great Britain at Rugby League. He never once shirked the exhausting demands on him to play both codes. Just two days after his outstanding performance for the RAF at Leicester, he produced a two-try performance for the Great Britain Rugby League team in their 27–8 triumph over France.

Murphy's next three international caps were won against the New Zealand tourists, in a series which Britain won 2–1 and made Murphy a certainty for his second tour of Australia in 1962. But 1961 still had more glory to offer Murphy apart from his exploits in the Great Britain and RAF teams. St Helens believed that with quality players like Murphy, Vollenhoven and Karalius, to name a few, they could match the best in the league. Already many good judges were tipping them as possible cup-winners. The Challenge Cup first round provided tough opposition as the Saints found themselves paired against Widnes. But with home advantage they felt reasonably confident of success. A packed Knowsley Road was left nervously contemplating the outcome after a ferocious struggle ended in a 5–5 draw. The speed of the St Helens backs, and of Murphy in particular, had been curtailed by a heavy muddy pitch.

The replay was at Widnes's Naughton Park ground on Thursday 16 February 1961. The game had fired the public's imagination and the gates were closed for the replay. Murphy was in his RAF position at stand-off. He felt confident. The ground was dry and firm and Murphy knew this would be to Saints' advantage with himself, Vollenhoven and Sullivan the quickest men on the field. At first Murphy applied a kicking policy which so unsettled the Widnes full-back, Pimblett, that he missed Vollenhoven as the Springbok flew in for a fifth-minute try. Then Murphy produced a superb reverse-kick with his back to the Widnes posts to send Sullivan over for a second try and St Helens were on the march.

Widnes hit back briefly with a try from the stand-off, Frank Myler, Murphy's half-back partner in the previous year's World Cup. Then Murphy decided to take control. The turning point came just before half-time. Murphy gathered a pass just outside his own 25 and accelerated away in a swerving run to take him clear of the incoming Widnes tackler. Once in full flight there was no stopping him as his electric pace took him 75 yards to the Widnes line for a magnificent touch-down which silenced the home crowd. Austin Rhodes converted and Saints led 14–3.

When Widnes rallied briefly with a Dawson try, which the player goaled himself, Murphy again stepped up a gear to disappoint Widnes. Breaking clear from two tackles, Murphy threw a long pass out to his right for Large to touch down. There was no stopping Murphy now. To crown a magnificent individual performance he rocketed from a scrum and powered his way through for his second try of the match. The Widnes players raised their arms in surrender and half in disbelief at his magic as he led Saints to a 29–10 victory.

So gallant Widnes, who had held St Helens 5–5 at Knowsley Road, finally succumbed to Murphy on their own ground. Curiously Wigan, like St Helens, almost fell at the first hurdle of the Challenge Cup. They also drew their first game 5–5 with Leeds before winning the replay. Neither club realized then that both would go on to reach Wembley. After their replay win, Wigan's international captain, Eric Ashton, went on a 'spying mission' to Naughton Park to watch the St Helens v. Widnes replay. After the game Ashton declared Murphy the best stand-off and scrum-half in the world. Ashton, who had led Great Britain in some memorable matches himself, wrote in a newspaper article: 'I've seen enough of Murphy to say that he has no superior in either position since the war.' The Widnes captain, Frank Myler, said of Murphy's performance in the Cup replay: 'It was sheer brilliance.'

Saints won their second-round clash at Castleford, 18–10, again helped by a decisive Murphy try, and went on to knock over Swinton in the quarter-finals. Murphy was again amongst the try-scorers against Swinton, as St Helens emerged 17–9 victors, in front of their own fans. The Swinton win put St Helens through to the semi-finals against a Hull team steeped in Wembley tradition. And Hull had an added incentive to reach Wembley again after finishing as losing finalists in the previous two years.

The big game was at Odsal Stadium, Bradford. The experts had made St Helens hot favourites for the semi-final, but at half-time there was a lot of hard talking in the Saints dressing-room. Hull had matched them tackle for tackle and Murphy's team only just had their noses in front at 5–4. In the second half Murphy's pace and touch-kicking, so often his main weapons in wearing down the opposition, did the trick again. Eventually St Helens ran out comfortable winners, 26–9, to book their place at Wembley for the third time in eight years. Meanwhile, Wigan had set up what was to be a classic Wembley final with victories over Wakefield Trinity, Salford and Halifax. Mighty Wigan, who'd won the Cup twice in the previous three years, boasted such an infinity of stars as the elegant Eric Ashton, Billy Boston, David Bolton (a former team-mate of Murphy's on tour in 1958) and Brian McTigue, all international tourists.

St Helens were led by the 'wild bull of the pampas', Vinty Karalius, and in Murphy and Vollenhoven, they had two of the quickest men in the game.

On Cup final day clear blue skies arched over the stadium, and the house was full. Aircraftman Murphy began the tactical battle in the tunnel before the teams marched onto the field, turning to Eric Ashton and saying: 'There's nothing down for you today, Eric, you're not quick enough.' Ashton was taken aback. Said Murphy later: 'I knew I had no equal from a standing start and warned Eric before the game.' Murphy had set his sights on his first Wembley winner's medal and was determined Wigan wouldn't spoil the party. He realized he would come in for heavy punishment early on and Wigan didn't disappoint him as twice he crashed to the ground from heavy tackles. But it was Murphy who sank Wigan on the half hour. Dick Huddart, Saints' eventual Lance Todd Trophy winner for the man-of-the-match performance, broke clear and passed to Murphy going at full throttle in support. The Saints roared as Murphy rocketed away, chased all the way to the line by the powerful Billy Boston. But no one could catch Murphy once he was in the clear and he touched down as Boston steamed behind him in a despairing run.

It was the first try of the afternoon and it proved crucial for St Helens. However, the game still hung in the balance with Saints 5–4 to the good and Wigan threatening to overpower them in the tackle. Then the Saints' centre three-quarter, Ken Large, linked with Vollenhoven in a run for the Wigan line. Large drew Ashton into the tackle and threw his pass out to Vollenhoven for the killer try. Saints had taken command of the game and went on to a memorable 12–6 victory.

Murphy, with an Australian tour and a Cup-winner's medal behind him, and a man-of-the-series performance for Great Britain in the previous year's World Cup, had reason to feel satisfied. He was still only twenty-two and enjoying his rugby as wholeheartedly as he did as a schoolboy.

But now there was to be a change of coach at Knowsley Road. The great Jim Sullivan, whom Murphy so admired, moved on and the player-coach, the valiant Alan Prescott, stood down in the autumn of 1961, Stan McCormick taking charge. A former teenage scrum-half with Oldham and the now defunct Belle Vue Rangers, McCormick had played for Great Britain and was on the wing when St Helens lost to Huddersfield in the 1953 final. He eventually won a winner's medal with Warrington the following year, after a replay with Halifax. McCormick could hardly believe how brilliant a player Murphy was. 'Murphy was the king pin at Saints. He was the inspiration for the whole team, the player everyone feared. Stripped, Murphy was a very powerful athlete. I was a professional sprinter but I can tell you he was explosive from a standing start. Once Murphy had gone through a gap it was all over. He could break from the half-way line and you couldn't stop him. People who tried, bounced off him. He was immensely powerful, almost like dynamite.'

McCormick also recognized Murphy's courage: 'He took a lot of stick because he went where the fire was. If he ran away it was because he had spotted a gap. He used to take on forwards, and there were some big men around. He was the best trainer I'd ever come across and that gave him his super fitness. Vinty Karalius was a powerful man and a good shield for Murphy. Vinty always looked after Alex during a game if he was getting stick. But, make no mistake, Murphy could knock people down himself because of his strength.'

McCormick also recalls training sessions at Knowsley Road: 'We used to practise drop-goals. Bob Dagnall would go acting half-back and turn the ball inside for Murphy to drop the goals. They could have done it blindfold, they perfected it that much. Murphy's reflexes were so quick that during matches opponents would give up tackling him if he attempted a drop-goal because the ball was usually on its way between the posts. You'll never see another like him.'

McCormick remembers, too, the great Jim Sullivan's influence on Murphy's earlier career: 'Sully encouraged him in every aspect of his play. When I got there he was a joy to handle.' Murphy also remembers: 'Sully used to tell me that if I was in an opponent's 25 I musn't come away without something. He used to tell me to drop a goal if a try wasn't on. It's an art.'

Murphy proved the point in a Saints match when he dropped three goals so quickly that it led to the league changing the rules to reduce a drop-goal's value to a single point. Murphy hit back: 'I'll drop twice as many.' He adds: 'I could think quicker than most players. It was a legitimate ploy. Why should it have been penalized?'

Murphy's sixteenth Great Britain cap came against France in February 1962. A faultless performance from him endorsed his selection for his second tour of Australia, one which threatened to end his playing career while he was still in full bloom.

Great Britain's 1962 tour of Australia and New Zealand started in controversial fashion for him when during the 39–12 victory over Western Australia, he was cautioned for criticizing the referee's handling of the game. His outburst made his name headline news in the Australian papers, and when the first Test was played at Sydney Cricket Ground on 9 June he was already a marked man.

However, despite rough punishment, Murphy's influence on the game was a key factor in Britain's win. Though he left the field for treatment after being concussed in a head-high tackle, Murphy showed the Australians he'd lost none of the class they had first seen in 1958 when he was a teenager. As he left the field after that first Test victory by 31–12, the Australian captain, Reg Gasnier, acknowledged his vital contribution to the British victory.

Murphy was in top form again just twenty-four hours after the first Test, scoring two tries as the tourists beat NSW North Coast 33–13, and a week later he was named man-of-the-match in a 22–17 win over a powerful Queensland team when Britain's loose forward, Derek Turner of Wakefield, was sent off.

It was ominous for the Australians as Murphy's outstanding performances continued with another great display in

Toowoomba, when his two tries helped Britain to win 36–12. A week before the vital second Test he produced another sparkling display as Britain overwhelmed North Queensland 47–14. The Australian press warned that the St Helens maestro would clinch the Ashes if he wasn't stopped.

At Brisbane on 30 June 1962, he confirmed the critic's view with a brilliant performance as Great Britain clinched the Test series with a hard-fought 17–10 victory. The Australian press was full of praise for Murphy's inspirational qualities when he sold two dummies before racing under the Australian posts for a morale-sapping try. Soon after Murphy had to limp out of the match with a badly bruised and swollen ankle, but by then the damage had been done.

However, the Australians restored some of their lost pride in the third and final Test in Sydney on 14 July which they won by a single point. It was a brawling game which ended in controversy. Derek Turner and Mick Sullivan were sent off but with Britain down to eleven men Murphy, despite an arm injury, scored a long-range solo try straight from a scrum, which had the Australians gasping.

That Test defeat angered the tourists who were determined to avenge themselves against the star-studded Sydney St George side. Nearly 60,000 were in the Sydney Cricket Ground for the match. Orchestrating play throughout, Murphy scored a magnificent try, with sheer pace taking him through the Australians' cover, and was named the game's best player as Britain won 33–5. But Murphy was to pay a heavy price. He sustained another arm injury and by the time the tourists had arrived in New Zealand for the second part of the tour he couldn't bend his arm.

A muscle expert in New Zealand said he could get Murphy fit again but it proved to be a false promise. Stan McCormick remembers the agony he was in when he returned home. The initial damage had been done in the final Test when an Australian player hit his right arm in a tackle, bruising it from bicep to wrist.

McCormick accompanied Murphy's wife, Alice, to Manchester airport to meet him when he returned home. As he walked into the airport lounge Murphy said: 'My international career is over. My arm has gone.' The following day McCormick went with Murphy to see a specialist in St Helens. 'I told the specialist that Murphy felt his international career was finished,' says McCormick. 'The specialist turned to me and said: "His whole rugby career is finished." I knew Murphy's injury was serious because he couldn't bend his arm. It was locked solid.'

But everyone reckoned without Murphy's determination and will to play again. Rugby was his life and he wasn't going to give in easily. An operation followed in which a piece of bone, which had been growing through the muscle, was taken from his arm. With his right arm virtually useless, Murphy thought that his days in the RAF would be over, and expected an early release. He was mistaken. RAF Haydock had other duties in mind for him and he was seconded to greenhouse duty, instructed to spray the tomatoes and other vegetables. His young daughter, Ann, eased the pain with the succinct comment: 'My dad's fighting the greenfly.' And so the all-action Murphy ended his national service at Haydock's RAF camp spraying tomatoes. He was amongst the last servicemen to be stationed there and one of the last League players to have pulled on a Union jersey for the RAF: 'I'm very proud of that,' he says.

4

Australia Awaits

The mid-1960s were to bring more triumphs for Murphy whose international reputation was by then unchallenged after two successful overseas tours. But as his love affair with St Helens reached breaking-point, he was often on the verge of despair. In October 1963 Murphy gained his twentieth international cap against Australia at Wembley and was in the Great Britain team a month later against the tourists at Swinton. His career was blooming and more caps followed against France and New Zealand as he continued to claim the scrum-half position as his own.

His testimonial season, 1965–66, was the most spectacular in his ten-year reign at the club. Murphy, the international captain, had already led the Saints to four major cup victories including the Challenge Cup at Wembley. After that game, as Murphy took the cup from the hands of the Prime Minister, Harold Wilson, Harry Cook hugged his young captain: both men needed to win and they were sharing yet another moment of glory for the Saints.

But bitterness was soon to engulf Murphy. A season which had started with high hopes and had reached a dream conclusion was soon to turn into a nightmare. There was no hint of the drama to come when Murphy gained his twenty-sixth international cap for Great Britain in March when they beat France at Wigan's Central Park. He didn't realize it at the time but that was to be his last international appearance as a Saints player.

Saints' successful Wembley campaign began with a surprising 10–0 win over Wakefield Trinity at Belle Vue, only a week after losing to the same Wakefield side in the league. Murphy led his team superbly though the sides slugged it out for an hour before the first points were on the board; then Saints' South African goal-kicker, Len Killeen, landed a 25-yard penalty. As the wind whipped up in their faces Murphy used the conditions to push Wakefield back into their own 25 with some excellent touch-kicking. Then Murphy rammed home the advantage, setting up a try for Vollenhoven to secure victory for Saints. Murphy, though delighted with the win, was unhappy at centre while a new signing, Tommy Bishop, played in his favourite scrum-half position.

In the second round of the Challenge Cup, Saints beat Swinton 16–4 at Knowsley Road. Murphy was again conspicuous with his speed and touch-kicking, ensuring that Saints had the edge throughout. But Murphy was still playing at centre three-quarter and not liking one minute of it.

In the quarter-final against Hull Kingston Rovers, he was back in the half-backs at stand-off and helped to create one of the most dramatic finishes to a game ever seen at Knowsley Road. The young Saints captain pulled the game out of the fire when all seemed lost. Trailing 7–10, and with normal time running out, Hull KR conceded a penalty with their fans already cheering a famous victory. The kick was awarded after a flare-up deep in Rovers territory which saw Saints reduced to twelve men when the referee, Eric Clay, sent off their big prop-forward, Cliff Watson. Murphy realized that Saints were on the brink of defeat as the game moved into injury time and decided on desperate measures.

Aiming a perfectly weighted up-and-under kick through the Hull KR defence, he sprinted after the ball at full speed. As his high kick dropped behind the Rovers line, so Murphy pounced for the touch-down a split second before he was flattened by several players plunging for the ball. Eric Clay looked at the heap of bodies unable to see what had happened. The big crowd went silent as Clay consulted both his linesmen. Then he turned and signalled a try which was greeted by a deafening roar from the home fans. Len Killeen stepped up with the scores level for the kick under the posts. It looked easy but, in the tense atmosphere, needed a cool head. Killeen was equal to the situation and St Helens had grabbed a sensational victory in the third minute of injury time.

Hundreds of Saints' fans were unaware of the result after leaving the ground before the end, certain that their team had been beaten. Then even more drama was to unfold. In the boardroom Harry Cook and his directors were trembling with relief. Mrs Iris Hunter remembers the night clearly. 'I was looking after refreshments that evening and knew that Hull Kingston Rovers were winning with the game virtually over. In the boardroom Harry Cook turned to me and said, "We've had it." I said, "Nonsense, we'll win in the last minute." Harry Cook told me, "You're a bloody optimist." When he saw Alex kick the up-and-under and score, Cook nearly collapsed.

'The Hull Kingston Rovers directors wouldn't come in for refreshments after the game,' Mrs Hunter remembers, 'they were so disappointed. They were complaining furiously about the referee playing three minutes over normal time. But, make no mistake, Alex won us that match. He's been a law unto himself since he was a little boy. He wasn't scared of anyone, big or small, and never showed any signs of nerves on a big occasion. When Alex walked on to a field, you knew he was out for business. He was always exciting to watch. I liked him.'

Though St Helens started firm favourites for the semi-final against Dewsbury at Swinton's Station Road, they were made to struggle before winning. In the end it was Len Killeen's accurate kicking that won the game with two tries and three goals, as nerve-ends began to fray in the Saints' camp. And so

St Helens were through to their fourth post-war Wembley final; and this time it was to be a repeat of the 1961 meeting with the old enemy, Wigan, as their opponents.

Wigan's hooker, Colin Clarke, was suspended for the final. Wigan had no recognized replacement, which was a weakness Murphy knew could be exploited to the full. 'I told the lads before the final that without an experienced hooker Wigan would have to run after us for ball possession. That suited me down to the ground. We were superbly fit and Wigan were not going to match us on that score. 'We ran them hard and tackled them out of sight. It was easier than I thought it would be,' a view reflected in the score-line of 21–2 in St Helens's favour.

At twenty-seven, Murphy was now in his playing prime: he was captain of a team which had just won four major trophies and he was at the zenith of his international powers. He should have been a happy man. But though he kept up appearances, inwardly Murphy was fretting about having to play at centre three-quarter. 'I was the Great Britain scrum-half and many good judges kept telling me I had no equal anywhere in the world as a half-back. Yet St Helens insisted on playing me at centre,' says Murphy.

He discussed the situation with his wife, Alice, who is pretty knowledgeable about Rugby League, and she sympathized with his feelings: 'Alex believed, like Vollenhoven, that playing in the centre you would not get enough of the ball or of the action.' For a man accepted as the world's best scrum-half, it was a situation Murphy could tolerate no longer. So, after much soul-searching, he decided to refuse to play in the centre and so was set on a collision course with his club. The clash between club and player was now out in the open and at once Murphy began to be linked with one or another Australian club, where he was much admired after two brilliant tours.

However, the 1966–67 season got underway with Murphy still a Saints player although he was now out of the team. The final breaking-point was reached after a few weeks when he was refused training facilities at Knowsley Road. The club he'd been with since a boy, and with whom he'd won every honour in the game, suddenly shut the door in his face. Murphy was devastated.

During September he trained alone in a local park with just a few autograph-hunters to keep him company. However, when the novelty of training alone had worn off, he began to feel like an outcast. After much agonizing and many discussions with Alice, Murphy, unable to bear any longer the loneliness and lack of involvement in the game, decided on a move which was to end his association with St Helens. He sent in a written transfer request. So, just a few months after he had received a benefit cheque of £2,000 and had captained the side at Wembley, Murphy was now the forgotten man at Knowsley Road so far as team selection was concerned. Then he had another shock. The club slapped a huge £12,000 fee on his head and promptly listed him. The move stunned Murphy. There was no attempt at reconciliation and it was clear that the club wanted him to go.

The Saints fans on the terraces were in turmoil about the thought of losing their best player. 'Some people felt I should have been willing to play anywhere for the club and accused me of disloyalty. But I had played out of position many times in the team's interest. Other people felt I was absolutely right to take a stand on the issue when I was first-choice scrum-half for Great Britain.' The situation now looked hopeless from Murphy's point of view, and to join an Australian club seemed the only way out of the mess. The St Helens board felt the same and started negotiations with a top Australian club, North Sydney.

The row over whether he should play out of position at centre had, of course, been merely the catalyst of a problem which had been engulfing Murphy on and off the field for some time. It was a highly complex situation which had ramifications throughout the St Helens club. If Murphy had his loyal supporters, his outspoken and abrasive manner had made him a number of enemies.

His coach in the early 1960s, Stan McCormick, was definitely a Murphy-admirer. 'You could not find a better trainer anywhere. He was so keen to do well and had such natural ability to go with it. It was a joy to work with him and watch him on a rugby field.' But McCormick remembers the pressure he was placed under to play Murphy out of position on the wing: 'I believed that was wrong. Once Murphy had passed the ball he would have been out of the game. Playing him on the wing would have meant he'd be relying on everybody else. He was too good for that. I certainly wasn't going to put the best scrum-half in the world out of the game.' McCormick stuck to his guns and told his bosses he was unwilling to move Murphy from half-back: 'I once played Alex at centre and explained the reason to him. We were stuck with injuries to players and wanted a winning bonus. He didn't like it but accepted it once I'd explained things to him.'

McCormick remembers the arm injury Murphy suffered on the 1962 Australian tour and its effect on him when he returned home: 'I took the team captaincy off him because it was affecting his play. I wanted him to concentrate on his play without the worry of captaincy. He certainly wasn't a hundred per cent fit when he came back from the tour. But if the board had held a gun to my head and said you must do this or that I would have told them to pull the trigger. I knew at the time there were people who wanted Murphy on the transfer list. But he was the greatest asset we had. Murphy was a better player in training than some other players were during matches.'

Eventually it was McCormick who was given the sack after a defeat at Castleford. 'I was told my contract wasn't going to be renewed. They didn't like the word 'sack' but when I asked if I would be with the club the following season, they said "No". To me that was the sack.' However, McCormick still remembers his days at St Helens with a warm glow: 'It's a great club with great fans and we certainly had great players. Murphy, Vollenhoven, Karalius and others. For me they were the last really true professionals.'

Paradoxically, despite the bitterness that had begun to sour their relationship, Murphy's greatest admirer was still the man who had brought him to the club as a teenager – Harry Cook. Cook knew that Murphy would be hurt when the club bought Tommy Bishop from Blackpool as the team's first-choice scrum-half: 'Tommy Bishop was a good 'un but he wasn't as good as Alex,' admits Cook. 'I was upset myself when we bought Bishop. We bought him because some of my fellow directors were upset at Alex's attitude towards them and his outspoken remarks to them. Alex often told some of them that they didn't know anything about the game. I could have transfer-listed him then, but I wanted him to stay. I knew he didn't like playing at centre. And I also knew that he was without doubt the best scrum-half in the world. But he upset a lot of people, and something had to be done.'

Cook felt he had been driven into a corner. 'I had a good, hard-working board of directors and felt I just couldn't let them down. They wanted Bishop and felt something had to be done about Alex's attitude towards them. They had really reached breaking-point on the issue. Alex was so impulsive. He just couldn't control his tongue, and was spoilt because he knew he was the best scrum-half in the world. 'In every other way he was a terrific lad. And he was certainly too good to cast on one side.' And so the row over whether Murphy should play centre or on the wing or in the half-backs had its origins off the field in Murphy's outspoken clashes with the directors. Events moved rapidly that autumn. While Harry Cook was negotiating Murphy's transfer to North Sydney, Murphy and his wife agonized over whether they wanted to emigrate. Harry McKinnon, president of the North Sydney club, was keen to sign Murphy whose prestige and standing in the game in Australia was enormous. He had no doubts at all about Murphy's ability; he was much more concerned about the size of the transfer fee of £12,000, which would certainly be a world record.

The North Sydney supporters begged the club to do all in its power to get Murphy to sign for them and when St Helens agreed to reduce the fee, McKinnon got the nod. A lucrative four-year contract was on its way to St Helens for Murphy to sign, making him the most expensive and highest-paid player in the game. The ball was now in Murphy's hands. All that was needed was for him to put pen to paper. But the saga had yet another twist in store for a bemused rugby public.

Murphy and Alice were now reconciled to the inevitable and decided to emigrate. 'We had a sailing date and were to take my mother and father with us to Australia,' Alice Murphy remembers. A 'For Sale' notice was posted outside their house in Thatto Heath and, with emigration plans virtually complete, Murphy and his family awaited the arrival of the contract from North Sydney. 'We had been told that the streets of Sydney were paved with gold,' recalls Alice. 'I remember the contract arriving and discussing with Alex whether we should sign it. Suddenly, I said to him, as he lifted the pen, "Do you want to go?" He replied, "Do you?" I said, "Not really." Alex replied, "Neither do I!" '

And so at the very last moment the Murphys decided against the move. Alice remembers: 'Alex tore up the contract and threw it on the fire. If he'd signed, we would have burned our boats. We were very happy apart from the rugby situation, and by leaving England we had a lot to lose.' Murphy was sad but was sure he'd done the right thing: 'Australians are my kind of people. They play to win. It's a wonderful country, and I have many good friends there, but when it came to the crunch I didn't really want to leave St Helens.'

Meanwhile in Sydney, Harry McKinnon, unaware that Murphy had changed his mind, was explaining to the North Sydney fans why the club had moved in for Murphy. McKinnon was confident that the outstanding skills and ability that all had seen on Murphy's two successful tours of Australia would pay for his contract through increased gate money. McKinnon boasted: 'Murphy will draw big crowds all over Australia when he's playing.'

It was a sentiment shared by many people in the English game, but the size of the transfer fee had kept interested clubs away from St Helens's door. Everyone, that is, except Jack Rubin, the chairman of Leigh, a less fashionable club, only a few miles from Knowsley Road. Rubin, who had long been an admirer of Murphy's talents, suddenly moved in with a dramatic bid to keep Murphy in the British game, offering him a five-year contract as Leigh's manager and coach. Murphy at once accepted and became the highest-paid team-manager and coach in the game. But of course he could no longer play. That was a dreadful blow for St Helens. If Murphy stopped playing, Saints would not receive a penny for their biggest asset. Indeed, in this last curious twist, the biter was now being well and truly bitten. But the real losers were the fans as Murphy gave up playing at the peak of his career to concentrate on management.

5
Glory at Hilton Park

The contrast between St Helens and Leigh couldn't have been more pronounced. Champagne corks had been popping at Knowsley Road at the end of the 1965–66 season while flat beer was the order of the day at Hilton Park. Murphy's acrimonious departure from Knowsley Road after ten outstanding seasons, had left a bitter taste in his mouth but he was determined to re-establish his career somewhere.

Meanwhile Leigh had ended their season on the same dismal note it had began with: defeat at home. The fans were staying away and the Leigh directors were under fire. In a desperate bid to improve matters the club had even brought in a top middle-distance runner, Eric Haslam, a local man, to improve fitness. The club generally was at a low ebb. However, Murphy's much-publicized row with St Helens and his plans to emigrate to Australia were being closely monitored by the Leigh directors, particularly by their millionaire chairman. Rubin believed that Murphy's genius could save Leigh from going aground.

When Murphy agreed to join Leigh, Rubin and his board were ecstatic. 'It's not a gimmick,' said the jubilant Leigh chairman, 'it's a serious attempt to bring an outstanding personality to Hilton Park, keep Murphy in the game and hopefully put Leigh back at the top.' But obviously Murphy's arrival cast doubt over the future of Leigh's chief coach, Gerry Helme, the former Warrington scrum-half and the only player to win two Lance Todd Trophies at Wembley for being the best player on view in the 1950 and 1954 finals. Saturday 8 October 1966 was the day that Murphy's career took this unexpected turn when he went to Jack Rubin's office to sign his five-year contract. Three days later he was introduced to the players before taking charge of his first training session. He told them bluntly: 'I believe in fitness, hard training and hard work. Anybody letting me down in those areas will be out of the team.'

Management Murphy-style had begun and Hilton Park was to be turned upside-down in his quest for glory. To those who knew him well his approach had the stamp of himself as a player and the stamp of the man who moulded Murphy in his early days at St Helens – the great Jim Sullivan, who had always demanded hard work and peak fitness from his players. 'Sully believed the game was for hard men. He drove you hard,' recalls Murphy. Sullivan, by now an ailing man, had instilled into Murphy that there were no easy options. Success would only come through hard work and dedication. The Leigh players were about to learn that same lesson.

The so-called 'Murphy affair' had sent shock waves through the game. The rule book seemed to have been bypassed. On the one hand St Helens couldn't sell their own player because Murphy was now a coach and involved only in management at Leigh. On the other hand, Leigh couldn't play him because Murphy was still on the St Helens playing register. Wigan had offered £5,000 for Murphy, Wakefield Trinity £7,000; and the Saints chairman had agreed to sell Murphy to North Sydney for £8,000. Leigh's intervention had thrown everything into turmoil, and there were recriminations all round. Harry Cook was furious: 'Those sods from Leigh approached him and I didn't like it,' he said later. 'Leigh offered us just £1,000 for him. I showed the Rugby League authorities proof that I was going to be paid £8,000 for him by North Sydney. It was a mess and I took legal advice.'

Accusations and counter-accusations came thick and fast in the months following Murphy's split with St Helens. One press report urged that the 'Alex in Wonderland' saga be brought to an amicable conclusion at least by the following year. One thing was certain, however: no one was going to get their prize capture away from Leigh. But that did not stop other clubs trying to capture Murphy's signature. Wakefield Trinity had gone to enormous lengths to lure him across the Pennines once it was clear that his split with St Helens was beyond repair. Alice recalls the inducements offered to get her husband to start a new career in Yorkshire: 'There was a very wealthy man in Wakefield who offered Alex a very good deal. We even went to his home. It was knee-deep in carpet, an absolutely beautiful place. Alex discussed terms with the man. We were shown plans for a lovely housing estate which was to be built overlooking a golf course. We were even asked to pick any house we wanted on the estate and that would be thrown in free of charge. And I was told there would be the chance of a teaching job as well. It was very tempting for us. But the big risk was the contract. It would have been a contract with this man personally and not with the club so we said "No". And anyway we had decided we didn't want to leave our home in St Helens.'

Leeds had also made an approach for Murphy's signature during his earlier days with St Helens: 'We went to a sponsored dinner at the Queen's Hotel in Leeds,' Alice recalls. 'During the meal I was told how good Leeds could be to players and their wives. Afterwards we went to the home of a Leeds director and were offered more inducements. They told us Alex didn't need to move from St Helens. He would be allowed to travel. But I knew Alex wouldn't have been happy. We really didn't want to leave St Helens.'

Within a fortnight of taking over at Leigh, Murphy found himself in the director's box watching his new team taking on his former friends from St Helens. The match had been presented as a chance for Murphy to put one over on his old club but just before the game he startled his supporters by dropping the Great Britain forward, Mick Martyn, and reshuffling his team. St Helens were without key players through injury but still looked too strong for Leigh. But on the night they were brushed aside, Leigh storming through to a 29–5 victory and inflicting on St Helens their heaviest defeat of the season.

The defeat at Leigh left the St Helens camp in even greater disorder. The directors flatly rejected overtures from Leigh for Murphy to be allowed to resume his playing career, insisting that Leigh's real intention in offering him a coaching appointment was to have him playing in their team eventually. They feared that Murphy's appointment opened the door for clubs to target players they wanted by offering them coaching jobs until such time as the selling club was forced to reduce the transfer fee. They argued, in other words, that a coaching appointment was merely a device to reduce transfer fees.

Now rumblings were heard at the headquarters of the Rugby Football League in Leeds. It had already been ruled that Leigh were guilty of misconduct in signing Murphy while he was still on the St Helens playing register and transfer-listed at £12,000. Now it was decided to leave the matter there. There were to be no further developments, and threats of legal action served only to make all the parties concerned tread warily.

The affair trundled on into 1967, with Jack Rubin still trying to get lifted the stop on Murphy's playing career. However his first season as manager-coach ended with a greatly improved team, and gates were up at Hilton Park. Eventually, in the summer of 1967, after nearly twelve months out of the game as a player, the bitter dispute ended with Leigh agreeing to pay St Helens £5,000 and Murphy being released by St Helens to start playing again.

As the 1967–68 season began, Murphy showed he'd lost none of his class with a brilliant try – his first points as a player for Leigh – and yet another man-of-the-match performance in his club's 19–12 defeat of Widnes in an evening match at Hilton Park on 22 August 1967. It was his way of warning the rugby world that he was back in business. It was a magnificent display in front of a big crowd and despite a painful rib injury which needed strapping to allow him to finish the game. Jack Rubin's decision to risk the club's future by gambling on Murphy's genius was about to bear fruit.

Murphy now had two aims: to get Leigh back to the top of the Rugby League table and to re-establish his international career. In 1966, he had already gained twenty-six Great Britain caps with St Helens, their second most-capped player behind Murphy's former captain, Alan Prescott, and he was now concentrating on winning a place on the forthcoming tour of Australia and New Zealand. His selection for that tour was thought to be a formality: it would be his third tour, a feat no player had achieved since the second world war and Alan Prescott shared that view. Indeed Prescott believed that Murphy should not only go on the tour but should go as captain, and he said as much when Murphy was still at St Helens. Murphy was in peak physical condition and at the time was captain of St Helens. Prescott believed that Murphy had the pedigree to be captain of the tourists: he had individual brilliance and inspirational qualities of leadership which would be brought out if he was made captain.

Murphy and the Great Britain team had been lifted by Prescott's courage during the 1958 tour to Australia and New Zealand. As Murphy recalled later: 'I've never seen the kind of courage Prescott showed in that second Test. We all knew he was in terrific pain at half-time. His forearm was fractured but he decided to stay on the field. His courage inspired all the lads. We just had to win that Test for Alan Prescott.'

These then were the leadership qualities which, eight years later, Prescott believed Murphy possessed. Prescott's was an important voice for the Great Britain selectors to take notice of. But he wasn't the only one. Another Great Britain captain, Eric Ashton, was now concentrating on his coaching job at Wigan. He had a clear view of Murphy's qualities: 'I fear him more than any other opponent I've ever come up against,' wrote Ashton. 'He's truly the best I've met in Rugby League. With one twist of the body, one burst of fantastic acceleration, he can turn a lost cause into a triumph.' So the weighty words of Prescott and Ashton, two former Great Britain captains, were thrown behind Murphy's tour claims.

Indeed, Murphy was no stranger to international captaincy. He'd led his country against France and showed he could hold himself in check if the situation demanded. That Station Road Test was remembered as a brawling affair in which the referee, Denis Davies, sent off Marcel Bescos, the French captain, who refused to leave the field. The game was abandoned but it had given Murphy valuable experience in a difficult situation as skipper.

Eventually, when the international selectors named the 1966 tour party, Murphy was included though not as captain, despite the big voices who had been pushing his claims. Murphy, who was then running a successful joinery business, eventually withdrew from the tour party amid accusations that it was sour grapes because he had been overlooked as captain. He denied the charge, insisting that his business commitments prevented him from going on tour. It was a decision which was to leave him in the international wilderness throughout his five-year stay at Leigh. Having decided against touring, Murphy concentrated on his business and his captaincy at St Helens. He didn't know then that within months his Saints career would be over and his playing days apparently at an end.

Once Murphy had resumed his playing career with Leigh in August 1967 he put thoughts of his bitter split with St Helens and his tour disappointment out of his mind. Later that season he showed he'd lost none of his old fire when he was sent off against the leaders, Bradford Northern, at Hilton Park. The referee, George Philpott, marched him to an early bath for a high tackle on Tony Price, when Leigh were leading. Without their player-coach Leigh succumbed to a 13–6 defeat while Murphy protested his innocence.

Murphy was capturing the headlines but, more important, his Leigh team were becoming a real force once again. One press report at this time described Murphy as the 'perfect leader' after his team beat a powerful Wigan side 14–6. Murphy again demonstrated his class, kicking four goals – one a long-range effort arrowed through the Wigan posts minutes after he'd been knocked unconscious – to the delight of a big Leigh crowd. It was the fifth consecutive game in which he had been named man-of-the-match.

During that 1967–68 season the Australian tourists were in England and watched a league match at Hilton Park mainly to see Murphy in action. Reg Gasnier, the Australian captain and coach, hadn't seen him since the previous tour four years earlier. Murphy treated his old adversary to the full range of his skills, setting up a superb try for his winger, Peter Ashcroft, and then drop-kicking two goals from seemingly impossible angles as Leigh beat Salford 15–9. After the game Gasnier fired a broadside at the Great Britain selectors: 'A player of Murphy's class never loses his ability. I'd have him in my team at full-back if I didn't want him at scrum-half' was Gasnier's devastating observation on Murphy who was again out of favour with the international selectors.

Murphy's leadership qualities were also in evidence in another fierce encounter against Hull Kingston Rovers. Playing with a suspected broken elbow – shades of his hero of Brisbane, Alan Prescott – he set up Leigh's first try for the second-row forward, Bob Welding, and kicked four goals to lead Leigh to a shock single-point victory, 14–13. Even the Hull crowd cheered him from the field.

The Leigh full-back, Tom Grainey, commented: 'Even a half-fit Murphy was better than most. He was superb against Hull Kingston Rovers.' But Murphy was becoming increasingly a marked man as teams tried to stop him dictating play during matches. In Leigh's 6–6 draw at Salford, for example, he was flattened by a late tackle as he burst from the blind side of the scrum. A brawl ensued and ended only when four policemen raced on to the pitch to intervene between the fighting players. It was after that match that the referee, Eric Lawrinson, made the memorable observation: 'I saw no reason to send anyone off.'

Murphy and his Leigh team continued to write the headlines. When he was recalled to the county team after being ignored for four years, he answered the selectors with three dazzling tries in the first half before he left the field injured. But Murphy had already done the damage in half a game as Lancashire regained the county title with a 30–10 win in Cumberland.

The sheer genius and consistency of Leigh's player-coach continued to astound friends and critics alike. And he was yet to be the architect of Leigh's greatest glory. This never-to-be-forgotten period in the club's history began in January 1971. On New Year's day, Leigh were overpowered at Leeds 28–10. A week later the draw for the Challenge Cup first-round ties was made. Leigh came out of the hat with a home draw against Bradford Northern. Was this an omen, the statisticians asked? Fifty years previously – in January 1921 – Leigh had beaten Bradford Northern in the first round of the Cup before going all the way to a final victory over Halifax 13–0 at Broughton before the final was moved to Wembley Stadium.

Another first-round tie against Bradford Northern in 1971 seemed too good an omen to miss, and the press latched on to its significance. Could it happen again that Leigh would go all the way? Most people scoffed at the idea as totally fanciful – except Murphy. 'We're the fittest team in the league and on our day can beat anyone. Cup football is about winners on the day,' he fired back.

On Sunday 24 January 1971 Murphy, despite a damaged ankle, led his side to a narrow 9–2 victory over Bradford Northern in the first round. On 20 February he again inspired Leigh to a sensational win at Widnes, one of the cup favourites. His full-back, David Eckersley, plunged over the Widnes line seven minutes from time to snatch a dramatic 14–11 win. Still no one really believed that Leigh could go all the way. The quarter-final clash was against Hull at Hilton Park on 7 March. Both sides locked horns in a titanic struggle before Leigh nosed home by 8–4 to reach the semi-final stage.

Three days later Leigh beat Wigan 15–3 in the league, only the second time that season that the powerful Wigan side had been beaten. Again Murphy was the inspiration behind Leigh, dropping three goals against Wigan as his team ran into top form. Victories over Swinton, Workington and Hunslet followed, and now the pundits were considering Leigh's Cup chances with more respect.

The Challenge Cup semi-final was at Wigan's Central Park against a strong Huddersfield team. Murphy's unfashionable Leigh were now only eighty minutes from their first visit to Wembley and their first Challenge Cup final for fifty years. The prophecy of the first-round win over Bradford Northern was about to be fulfilled. That was the firm belief of Murphy and his team, though when Leeds got through to the final it was thought there could be only one winner – the men from Yorkshire.

The Huddersfield semi-final lived up to its pre-match billing with no quarter given. Murphy drummed into his players that they could reach Wembley only if they gave maximum effort throughout the match. 'I had no worries about our fitness. And we had the players who could tackle all day. But we had to watch for careless mistakes, or Huddersfield would cash in. My lads were magnificent.' Leigh reached Wembley with a hard-fought but narrow 10–4 win in a match which was in doubt until the final hooter. But they paid a heavy price. Their class forward, David Chisnall, was sent off by the Yorkshire referee, Billy Thompson, for a stiff-arm tackle, and his subsequent four-match ban was to cost him his place at Wembley. Murphy had plenty to say to Billy Thompson in the tunnel after the match, knowing how big a loss Chisnall would be: 'Chissy was only a young lad and quick-tempered on the field. I told Billy Thompson he wouldn't have had the bottle to send him off if it had been the final.' They were remarks that were to be thrown back in his face after the final, when events proved how wrong he was in his assessment of Thompson.

Leigh was now a town gripped by cup fever. There was much drum banging and trumpeting of their biggest sporting moment in half a century. Murphy was fêted wherever he went. And to show his confidence in his players he named his Wembley squad of nineteen almost immediately, an unprecedented move.

Murphy was worried that his remarks to Billy Thompson in the tunnel after the semi-final could cost him his Wembley place. How relieved he was when a disciplinary hearing decided that a warning was sufficient punishment and he was given the all-clear to play in the final against Leeds. Could Murphy, the man whose career had been rescued five years earlier by Leigh, now repay the club with Cup glory? Not even his closest friends thought it possible. Albert White, later to work with him at Warrington and at Salford where he became club director, had a big bet on Leeds: 'Leeds looked certainties. I lost a small fortune thanks to Mr Murphy and his team,' he joked. In fact Leeds were quoted at incredible odds of 5 to 1 on to win the Cup, making Leigh the longest-priced outsiders for many years. And Mrs Helen Smith, a Leigh spiritualist, had most people laughing when she said she had had visions of Murphy holding the cup after Leigh's victory.

However, Murphy, the super-optimist, had other ideas. Throughout the Cup run he was confident that Leigh was the fittest side in the league and could beat anyone on their day. And he'd already been a Wembley winner twice as a player with St Helens in 1961 and 1966. He was determined to make it a hat trick of victories.

Leigh obtained special permission to break with a Wembley tradition of no mascots, and four-year-old Gary Ashcroft, son of the Leigh and Great Britain hooker Kevin, marched onto the Wembley turf with the team. Murphy had told his players he wanted maximum effort from the start: 'We agreed that the best way to upset Leeds and the odds was to get at them straightaway and unsettle them. If we could get early points on the board I believed it would give us an important psychological advantage'.

It all worked out according to plan. Jim Fiddler responded with a third-minute drop-goal and then the former Swansea Rugby Union winger, Stuart Ferguson, added a penalty five minutes later. As Murphy had predicted, this early onslaught from Leigh rattled Leeds, who were clearly finding it difficult to get into their stride under a barrage of heavy first-time tackles from Murphy's men.

Murphy could sense Leigh were on the right course and mid-way through the first half he raced clear towards the

Leeds 25 and swung out a pass for Stan Dorrington to score from close range. Ferguson added the goal and Leeds were visibly rocking under the pressure. Murphy steadied himself and produced a superb drop-goal to take Leigh further ahead. On the point of half-time Ferguson added another penalty to give Leigh an astonishing 13–0 lead over a confused Leeds team whose rhythm had been destroyed by Leigh's tenacious approach.

In the dressing-room at half-time Murphy urged his players to more effort in the second half knowing they now had one hand on the Cup. Three minutes into that second half Leeds's teenage full-back, John Holmes, won their first points with a penalty and relief spread throughout the Leeds team. Murphy realized instantly that Leeds would be lifted and spotted his chance to drop another superb goal. It immediately rubbed out the Holmes penalty before Leeds could benefit from it. Then, Ferguson took advantage of another Leeds infringement and added two more penalty points for Leigh who were now leading 17–2 with just over twenty minutes left to play. Murphy was always in the thick of the action and the game was at breaking point for Leeds with time running out. Then with a quarter of an hour to go, the underlying tensions exploded, and it was Murphy who provided the spark. He dashed into the Leeds 25 as the Leeds skipper, Syd Hynes, closed in on him for the tackle.

What happened next created the most talked about moment in the history of Rugby League Cup finals at Wembley. Murphy crashed to the ground and lay motionless on the Wembley turf. A touch-judge raced onto the pitch to speak to the referee, Billy Thompson. Then the unthinkable happened. As Murphy was being carried off on a stretcher, Thompson dismissed Syd Hynes from the field, the first-ever player to be sent off in a Rugby League final at Wembley.

As the game restarted, Leigh rubbed salt into Leeds's wounds when Eckersley dropped a goal, then scored a try converted by Ferguson. Leigh now led 24-2 with just five minutes left for play. Leeds were faced with an impossible task but got a late consolation try from Wainwright, with Holmes adding the goal. Leigh finished easy winners 24–7 and the biggest Cup favourites in years had been toppled.

Arguments about the Hynes incident at Wembley have raged ever since. Billy Thompson dismisses claims that he was 'conned' by a piece of Murphy play-acting. He still vividly remembers the occasion: 'I didn't see the incident. The crowd roared and I turned to see what was going on. The touch-judge had come on and Murphy was lying on the floor. This had happened on the side of the pitch nearest to the Royal Box. The touch-judge told me Syd Hynes had viciously butted Murphy. I'd already spoken to Syd on two previous occasions during the match when he'd had a go at two other players and warned him that he would be dismissed next time. When the touch-judge said Hynes had given Murphy a vicious head butt, what was I supposed to do? I wasn't interested in Murphy. I'd already warned Syd Hynes twice. That was good enough for me. It was good-night for Syd this time. I pointed and said to him, "Dressing-room", and Syd walked off.'

It was a decision which Billy Thompson has had to live with ever since. But he insists it was the right one. Following the final Thompson receiving dozens of letters from clubs supporting his decision to send off Hynes. 'They praised me for having the guts and courage of my convictions.' One newspaper headline described him as 'Billy the Brave'. In fact, many of the arguments about whether Murphy had 'conned' the Cup final referee were derived from newspaper articles written by Murphy before the final when he had criticized Thompson.

Thompson smiles as he recalls the moment when the Leeds and Leigh teams waited in the Wembley tunnel before going out on to the pitch. 'In the tunnel outside the dressing-rooms Murphy patted me on the back and said, "Are you all right, sir?" If Murphy felt that by patting me on the back and calling me "sir" it would make any difference to the game, he was greatly mistaken. Indeed, if I had allowed myself to be influenced at all by this familiarity my decision in the Hynes incident would have gone the other way'.

After the game Thompson bravely took up an invitation to

attend the club's reception at the Park Lane Hotel. 'The Leeds people were naturally distressed about having their captain sent off. But they admitted to me they had lost to a better team. Leigh were the underdogs but they were brilliant that day. I remember the speed of their first try. Murphy put a long pass out to Stan Dorrington to score. The pass was absolutely brilliant, missing out three players to send Dorrington in. Murphy won the Lance Todd Trophy that day as the game's outstanding player. He was tremendous.'

Murphy insists he was kidding no one over the Hynes incident. Suggestions that he was play-acting infuriate him. 'I saw Syd coming in for the tackle. I woke up in the bath. That's the next thing I remember. He certainly caught me.' Thompson adds: 'If he kidded anyone that afternoon then he kidded everybody. The St John ambulance people put him on the stretcher.'

Murphy scoffs at stories that have since embellished the incident: 'I've heard stories that I was winking when they put me on the stretcher. I might have been blinking but I certainly wasn't winking. I'm supposed to have told them which substitute to send on while I was being carried off. It's nonsense. Syd was a very good professional and a good pal of mine off the field. Leeds were 5 to 1 on and he wanted to win. Maybe he didn't think he'd caught me as hard as he did but let me tell you this, and if you don't believe me ask the Wembley doctor. Ask him what I was like in the dressing-room. Just before the end of the game I struggled back on to the field to take the Cup and then nearly dropped it coming down the steps after the presentation. I didn't know what year it was. I went back to our hotel and went straight to bed. People thought I'd conned Billy Thompson because we'd had a run-in when he sent off David Chisnall in the semi-final against Huddersfield. It's true I had a go at him in the tunnel after that game and told him he'd "bottle out" at Wembley. That's why some people thought I'd conned him. But they forgot that Billy told me straight in the tunnel after the Huddersfield game, "I'll do my job, you do your job, and mind your own business." You couldn't kid Billy Thompson.'

Murphy and Billy Thompson had crossed paths many times in their careers before Wembley 1971. And Thompson was fully aware of Murphy's reputation for 'kidding' referees. He recalls a match at Wigan when the Leigh hooker, Kevin Ashcroft, shouted to him that Murphy had been knocked out. 'Murphy was lying on the floor and the Leigh trainer came on. I said, "There's nothing wrong with him", and sent the trainer back off. I then turned to Ashcroft and said, "I bet he gets up to feed the scrum." I knew Murphy was a kidder and that's why it didn't come into the question at Wembley when I sent off Syd Hynes. The thing with Murphy was that he was a winner, and if he could get away with anything he would try. But I wasn't kidded by him or anyone else at Wembley. The touch-judge saw what happened and I acted accordingly.

'When you play against the Australians you have to have characters like Murphy to beat them,' Thompson insists. 'Murphy was a great player. He could bring people through a gap, chip the ball and run on to it if opponents were getting on top of him; and he could swing a game with his superb touch-kicking, and could dominate a game because he had a marvellous Rugby League brain. He was still outstanding in his thirties when he joined Warrington, but he wasn't as good as he was at St Helens. There, no one could touch him.'

On one occasion referee Thompson fell foul of Murphy's admirers. One Murphy fan was a Catholic priest, he recalls: 'Father Sefton from St Mary's sent me a four-page letter complaining about my attitude to Alex Murphy. He told me that other people let Murphy get on with the game. "But you go out of your way to prove that you are the boss," he wrote. And he told me he wished he had 200 Alex Murphys in his parish. I think he liked Alex!

'But you had to get in first with Alex, otherwise he would run the game. He was volatile and would have a go. He was a bag of tricks. When he played scrum-half at Leigh he was the finest "feeder" of a scrum you've seen. But if you caught him "feeding" he never complained or denied it. I might add he didn't always put the ball in straight,' laughs Thompson. 'But you could have all the aggro in the world with him and he would be the first to buy you a drink after a match and forget it. There's been no better player of the game or bigger character.'

If Billy Thompson admired Murphy's exceptional skill and speed as a player, he also respected his other qualities as well. 'He was as hard as nails and had courage. He took plenty of stick but I never heard him moan about it. He had to take some beatings because he was a marked man. Murphy liked hungry players and players with fire in them like Ashcroft and Chisnall at Leigh. And, whatever his critics say, you can't beat his record.'

Thompson recognized that Murphy was often in trouble with officials but springs to his defence: 'He was always controversial because if you asked him a question he didn't cut corners. He told you straight what he thought. That got him a bad name when really people should have admired him for it.' Sometimes even Billy Thompson came in for Murphy's straight talking. Once Leigh were beaten in a cup-tie by Castleford at Hilton Park. Billy Thompson had refereed the game: 'Murphy went wild after that game. He told the commissionaire not to let me into the Leigh tea-room after the match. He accused me of not giving an off-side during the game. He told me straight that everybody thought I'd had a stinker. He looked me in the eye and said,"Nobody thinks you had a good game, Billy." I said to him, "One bloke here thinks I'm the best referee he's seen." Murphy said,"Who?" I said, "The chairman of Castleford: he's just shaken my hand." '

Thompson also remembers the disagreements he had with Murphy, but put up with them because of Murphy's brilliance as a player. 'Anybody who thinks he's not been good for the game has got it wrong. They're talking nonsense. He was a marked man and had to be a good 'un. He was a law to himself. There were always disputes when Murphy was playing. But you tell me a greater character or player who has emerged since he hung up his boots.'

Thompson also remembers when Murphy controlled himself: 'I remember a match at Batley when he was absolutely magnificent. He scored about three tries and dropped a couple of goals. Afterwards the man-of-the-match award was given to the Batley scrum-half, Tony Gorman. Murphy never complained.' And there was Murphy's witty side: 'In a match at Leigh, Murphy passed the ball to Frank Wilson whom he had recently signed. Wilson dropped it. Murphy came racing down the field and said to Wilson, "Here we are lads, £10,000-worth of rubbish." I think that was his confidence booster for Wilson. But make no mistake, a lot of people in the game respect Alex Murphy but they won't admit it. So I'll say it loud and clear: he is the best player and coach Great Britain has ever had.'

6
Hero and Villain

On Sunday 16 May 1971, following the great victory over Leeds, Alex Murphy returned home to a hero's welcome. A vast crowd of 50,000 squeezed into the Leigh town centre as news spread like forest fire that the open-top bus bringing home the Leigh players was approaching. It was a unique day for the club. Never before had the Leigh colours flown victorious after a Wembley final. On their very first visit to Wembley the army of fans had seen an impossible dream come true.

Banners proclaimed: 'Murphy the Magnificent' and 'Murphy's Wembley wonders'. Players, fans and club officials were riding high in the sky, not knowing that a storm was about to engulf them. Within days, Murphy's adoring fans were branding him 'traitor' and 'liar' when sensationally he left the club to join Leigh's neighbours, Warrington. One of Rugby League's best-kept secrets was now a matter for public debate.

Unknown to the Leigh fans who had journeyed to London and back on that triumphant Cup final weekend, officials of both clubs had been bonded together in secrecy, sitting on the time-bomb of Murphy's impending departure from Leigh. When it exploded on the unsuspecting fans, the fall-out was widespread.

Murphy recalls angrily: 'Leigh let me take the rap. The spekkies had a real go at me. What they didn't know was that the club chairman, Jack Harding, who had not long taken over from Jack Rubin, and his fellow directors knew all along that I was leaving but wanted it kept quiet while we were still involved in the Cup-run. I was made out to be the villain of the piece and I was accused of being two-faced with the fans. But what could I do when the directors wanted everything kept quiet until our run was over? When we returned home with the cup that Sunday afternoon the welcome the fans gave us brought tears to my eyes. The players could hardly believe it. It was a very emotional moment for us all. 'Can you imagine what would have happened if I'd announced on the Town Hall steps that I was leaving the club? There'd have been a riot.'

If Murphy felt that discretion was the better part of valour on that history-making Sunday afternoon, in front of massed fans, his part in what was dubbed the 'Wembley conspiracy' was to leave a bitter taste in the mouths of his admirers.

He insists to this day: 'I didn't let anyone down at Leigh. I told Jack Harding after the second round of the Cup that I'd been offered the Warrington job if I wanted it. And to prove my loyalty to Leigh I told Warrington that as long as Leigh were involved in the Cup, I would not consider leaving Hilton Park. But it was known for weeks before the final that I could be joining Warrington. I think Jack Harding and his board of directors sold the Leigh fans down the river.'

A Warrington director, Brian Pitchford, later to become chairman, recalls how the dilemma was unfolding during the Leigh Cup-run which was to take them all the way to Wembley that May: 'Leigh's chairman, Jack Harding, contacted our chairman, Ossie Davies, and asked if we could come to some agreement on the Murphy situation because he felt it would "burst the balloon" if it became known that AJ was leaving Leigh.' He was particularly keen that Warrington should keep quiet until after the Wembley final. 'Harding asked us not to make any official announcement about Murphy joining us at Warrington until at least the Thursday following the final in case there was a replay.'

In the event it was Murphy who was to feel the wrath of the fans, some of whom have never fully forgiven him for what they believed was a walk-out by him. The Cup hero of Hilton Park was to become the villain. Murphy believes he had no option: 'I didn't walk out on Leigh. I was sworn to secrecy about my Warrington move until we were finished with our Cup run. It lingered on because we went all the way and won the Cup. But Leigh's directors knew what was going on.' Even the signing of the contract taking Murphy from Leigh to Warrington was done with an air of considerable secrecy, broken only when the story appeared in the national press.

On Monday 17 May 1971, forty-eight hours after the Wembley victory, a meeting was held at the Greyhound public house in Leigh which was to change the course of Murphy's career. Present at that pub gathering were four key people besides Murphy: both club chairmen, Davies and Harding, Leigh's general manager, John Stringer, and the club's bank manager, Gordon Hulme, from the local Natwest branch. When the meeting broke up Murphy was no longer with Leigh, having signed a five-year contract taking him to Leigh's neighbours, Warrington.

Jack Harding was quick to go on record, saying that he'd offered Murphy a substantial contract to stay on at Hilton Park. 'Short of selling the ground it was the best offer we could make,' said Harding at the time. But Murphy claims Harding was holding back on a vital part of the sequence of events: 'I had become very attached to Leigh. After all, they had saved my career when I'd split with St Helens five years previously. After we had beaten Leeds in the final I told Jack Harding that the team would need re-building. I wanted a five-year contract to help keep the club at the top.'

Harding's response, claims Murphy, was a blow to his pride: 'He said to me, "How can you tell me the team needs re-building when we've just won the Cup?"' What finally decided Murphy, he claims, was Harding's assessment of him:

'He told me I had to prove myself as a coach. He said I'd proved myself beyond doubt as a player-coach but not as a coach in my own right.' Murphy was convinced where his future lay when Harding added that he didn't believe in long contracts for coaches but was prepared to give Murphy another three years at Hilton Park. 'Whatever he may have thought about my ability as a coach, Harding didn't want me badly enough to offer me a five-year contract,' says Murphy.

7
Wilderspool and No Regrets

In the week following Leigh's Wembley triumph Murphy was introduced to the Warrington public as the new man in charge of team affairs at their club. It was a strange turnabout. Murphy never regretted the move though he admits it was a big wrench to leave Leigh. But at Warrington 'Ossie Davies and Brian Pitchford were terrific directors to work for, and I had a great time with them. It's a part of my career I look back on with a great deal of pride, and don't forget we had a lot of success there as well'.

To this day Murphy counts Brian Pitchford as one of his closest friends: 'He never broke his word to me if I asked for anything. I once let him down because I was misinformed about a certain matter. I had misread that particular situation and should have known better than to doubt Brian Pitchford.' There's no doubt that the two Warrington directors were delighted to have secured Murphy's services. Ossie Davies had warned a supporters' meeting weeks earlier that attendances had to improve at home matches if Rugby League was to be kept alive at Wilderspool. Murphy's Leigh team had beaten Warrington in the last home game of the 1970–71 season at

Wilderspool to complete a league double over them.

When Murphy signed his Warrington contract just over a month later, Ossie Davies told the Warrington fans it would bring back the good times to Wilderspool. He said that Murphy was the outstanding personality in Rugby League and the game's best coach, and he urged the fans to back the club at the turnstiles.

Ossie Davies and Brian Pitchford had been deeply depressed by the club's decline during the 1970–71 season. Gates had plunged alarmingly to as few as 1,000 to 1,500, and the club's debts were mounting. 'We were prepared to put forward a plan for injecting cash into the club, writing off the debts and putting money into development,' recalls Pitchford. But the plan depended on the other directors, including the chairman, Walter Challinor, resigning *en bloc*. Davies and Pitchford outlined their proposals to the next board meeting when it was fully discussed. An extraordinary general meeting was then called when the shareholders were asked to decide the issue. The Davies-Pitchford survival package was accepted and the old board stood down.

Pitchford takes up the story: 'I remember the previous season we had been beaten out of sight by Salford by 50 points. The situation was becoming desperate then. If we had not taken over and put money into the club it would have folded. I was prepared to do that along with Ossie Davies because we both knew the club had reached rock-bottom.'

The two men decided that their first priority after taking over was to bring in a top-flight coach, preferably with a big name. Alex Murphy fitted the bill perfectly. Pitchford had always been an admirer of Murphy after watching him as Great Britain's youngest-ever tourist in Australia in 1958. 'We let it be known on the grapevine that we wanted someone like AJ at Warrington,' Pitchford says. The grapevine worked. The two men met at Ossie Davies's home and talked with Murphy: 'We made an offer to AJ and he didn't haggle about it. It was a lucrative contract with full involvement in the club over five years. He asked us for complete control of the playing side and we gave it to him, which suited AJ down to the ground, I remember. Basically he had real control over the buying and selling of players. All we wanted in return was to be told what he was doing.

'Murphy was given a global figure to work within and we made it clear that we were not buying a dog and barking ourselves. We knew AJ was an excellent judge of players and we had mutual trust in our dealings with him. Mind you, it could have all gone horribly wrong from the start if we'd bought the players or picked his team for him. We left all the decisions on the playing side to him and I ran the business side with Ossie. I am chairman of my company and I would not spend half a million pounds on a piece of machinery without the advice of my engineering expert. We employed AJ as a Rugby League expert and encouraged him to get on with it.'

Despite limited success in his first season, Murphy had impressed his new bosses: 'The thing that struck Ossie and me in AJ's first season was how he coped with adversity. It didn't go well. It was no fault of AJ's judgement but things didn't go right for many reasons. We had injuries to key players, suspensions and the like, though we did reach the semi-finals of the Challenge Cup and that in itself was quite an achievement. But Murph impressed us most at that time and we never regretted for a moment bringing him to Wilderspool.'

If Davies and Pitchford did have any lingering doubts about the wisdom of their hiring Murphy, then Murphy himself quickly dispelled them. 'He told us that with two or three new players in his team jig-saw, he would crack it for us and bring success to the club,' says Pitchford. Murphy told his bosses that he needed players in three key positions to make Warrington a side capable of top honours: a centre, a winger and a loose forward. And he thought he might also need a hooker. As events unfolded over the next couple of seasons the assessment proved absolutely accurate.

One of the key factors in those developing halcyon days at Wilderspool was the fact that Davies and Pitchford had their hands firmly on the reigns of power and could come to decisions very quickly with no big board of directors to refer to. Pitchford points out: 'We used to hold board-meetings at the front of the team bus returning from matches if we had anything important to decide. We could make decisions on the spot.' Murphy remembers how much precious time this saved for him: 'They didn't have to call a full board-meeting. They were the board. I would often go to them with a problem and Ossie and Brian would hold a meeting there and then and give me a decision. I couldn't ask for more.' The board-meetings on the team bus had their humorous side, as Murphy remembers: 'Ossie would sometimes appear to nod off while you were talking to him. He'd still be smoking his pipe but you couldn't tell if he was asleep or not. Then he'd suddenly wake up and give you an answer to your problem. Those meetings were a tremendous help and saved a lot of time and hassle.'

Murphy also remembers the keenness and team spirit throughout the club. 'Everyone from Ossie and Brian down to the kit man, Ockher, and the tea ladies was made to feel important and the jobs they were doing valuable to the club's future. That's how good Ossie and Brian were at running the club. And they always stuck to their word so that you knew exactly where you were going.'

One of Murphy's first concerns after taking over was to organize his backroom staff. Tommy Lomax, a former featherweight boxing champion who worked in the club's leisure complex as a massage man, was brought in by Murphy to co-ordinate training sessions. 'Tommy had the expertise from his professional days in the ring and I needed him to sharpen the players' movements and responses. He did a superb job for me.'

Murphy left his players in no doubt where they stood and what he wanted from them. In typically blunt fashion he told them: 'I want each one of you to prove yourselves to me. As far as I'm concerned, there are no first-team players here. You have to show me that you're good enough to be selected for the first team. That first-team jersey's going to be worn with pride and it'll have to be earned.' And he had a message for the fans: 'Despite what some people may tell you, I don't perform miracles. And I can't guarantee success. But I can guarantee this: if maximum effort can bring success then we'll get there.

We'll be the fittest team in the league and we'll be one-hundred per-cent triers.'

His impact on the club was immediate and just what Davies and Pitchford had hoped for. The training school in that summer of 1971 attracted record numbers with a big turn-out of first teamers, the 'A' team, colts and schoolboys. The summer school was used by Murphy to get first impressions of playing strength and bring his players into proper condition for the coming season.

The first obstacle he encountered was predictable. If he wanted to sign a player the fee doubled. 'I was being quoted £10,000 for players who'd proved nothing with their own clubs. But if I fancied them, the clubs thought I'd seen something they hadn't. Some of the players looked like donkeys but I thought I could improve them. But not at the prices being quoted.'

Murphy gave notice of what the Warrington fans were in for in his first game for the club at Wilderspool. He dropped a goal – the first points he scored for the club and his hallmark throughout his career – scored a try and converted another in Warrington's victory over Whitehaven.

Then as the 1971–72 season got under way, he realized his squad needed strengthening. He swooped into the transfer market by going back to his former club Leigh for two players, the prop, Dave Chisnall, and second-row forward, Geoff Clarkson. The pair cost Warrington a bargain £12,000 and a flabbergasted Murphy was taken aback: 'They were Leigh's best players. Jack Harding agreed the fee and I think that ruined the Leigh team which I'd left behind. I was staggered at the price Leigh let them go for. Chissy (Dave Chisnall) was one of the best prop forwards in the game and still in his prime. He was very fast and had a good pair of hands with the ball. Geoff Clarkson I also knew very well. I'd signed him for Leigh from Bradford Northern and he'd done a good job for me at Hilton Park. I just couldn't believe that Leigh were prepared to let them go so cheaply.'

Chisnall was to make an instant impact at Warrington but not quite in the manner Murphy had in mind. In September

1971, Warrington drew 9–9 with Bradford Northern at Wilderspool. The match was a brawling affair with players injured in the fracas. The referee, Billy Thompson, sent off Chisnall and Parr, a dismissal which was to cost Chisnall a six-match ban when he appeared before a disciplinary hearing at the end of the month. Murphy, though, is quick to defend Chisnall: 'I don't think we were one of Billy Thompson's favourite clubs. Chissy was only a young lad and was a bit quick-tempered. He was a hard lad on the field but very placid off it. The ban on Chisnall really hit Warrington because he was a very good player.'

It was during these early days at Warrington that Murphy's international career was revived. He was selected to play for Great Britain at scrum-half in the second Test against the New Zealand tourists at Castleford. Murphy was to replace the first choice, Steve Nash of Featherstone, who had pulled out after being hurt in a freak accident while pushing a motorcycle which had broken down.

During that month, October 1971, Murphy returned with his Warrington team to his former club, Leigh, for a BBC Floodlit Trophy match. Warrington lost 6–2 and the Leigh fans let Murphy know what they felt by jeering him. The loudest jeer of the night came when Murphy kicked a penalty and then missed another from an easier position. The former hero of Hilton Park was again the villain.

It was at about this time that Murphy began again to suffer from pains in his arm. 'My right arm was giving me trouble and getting worse. I couldn't bend it and had to stop playing.' He was taken to Warrington General Hospital and there was operated on to remove a piece of bone in the muscle of his right elbow, a legacy of that 1962 tour of Australia when he was badly hurt in Sydney.

With Murphy in hospital the team struggled, losing to Halifax at home in the Players No. 6 Trophy after he had ordered wholesale team changes. Defeat after defeat followed at home and there were rumblings of discontent on the terraces. Murphy was concerned but knew he had the backing of Davies and Pitchford and was confident he could put things right. Then he returned, after missing a string of games, to lead his side in a 46–11 thrashing of Bramley, and followed that with victories over two other Yorkshire clubs, Featherstone and Hunslet, away; and their winning ways continued over Christmas with the 'double' over Hunslet at Wilderspool.

It was just the sort of form Murphy had been striving for as the first round of the Challenge Cup approached. The draw favoured Warrington with a home tie against Batley. They duly won that game comfortably by 30–7 and the Warrington boat was in calm waters again with Murphy at the helm. But a storm was coming: Murphy fell foul of the authorities.

Warrington won again against Oldham by a single point, 16–15, in February 1972. But the match went wrong for Murphy who was given his marching orders for illegal use of his elbow on Oldham's Frank Foster. He was in similar trouble again later the same month, the two offences bringing him a five-match ban.

The second occasion was during the Challenge Cup second-round match at Wheldon Road, against Castleford, which ended in a draw 8–8. Murphy saw little of the game. This time he was dismissed for a tackle on Castleford's international full-back, Edwards, who was carried off on a stretcher, after fifteen minutes. 'It was a hard cup-tie with a lot at stake,' says Murphy. 'I can't remember too much about it. I was in the bath most of the time.'

The following Wednesday the teams met again in the replay at Wilderspool when Warrington won 11–5 to earn a quarter-final place at Bramley. Warrington won the match at McLaren Field 14–7 and the town was buzzing with talk of Wembley, now only a tantalizing eighty minutes away and Murphy still in his first season at the club.

The Challenge Cup semi-final was against Murphy's old club, St Helens, and was to be played at neutral Central Park, Wigan. It was a game to fire the imagination and there was a massive demand for tickets. The Murphy magic was working well but ten days before the match Warrington were hit by a double injury blow. Their full-back, Derek Whitehead, and his team-mate, Mick Henighan, were injured in a car crash on their way to attend the wedding reception of another player, Bobby Wonbon. Brian Pitchford believes the accident cost Warrington their place in that year's Wembley final.

'We drew that first semi-final against St Helens 10–10,' Pitchford says, 'but I believe we could have won if Whitehead had been playing. Tobias du Toit, our stand-in goal-kicker in Whitehead's absence, scored a marvellous try from fifty or sixty yards out. But he failed with his conversion kick which would have given us victory. I'm sure Whitehead had the extra kicking ability to have landed that conversion attempt.' Murphy who brought his team to the peak of condition, had believed all along that Warrington would win the Cup. When told of the car crash involving his two players he was dismayed: 'I could hardly believe it. I was thoroughly dejected and very angry about the whole thing.'

The replay took place at Central Park four days after the drawn semi-final. With the teams level after another bruising match it looked as if another meeting would be needed to decide who went to Wembley. Murphy recalls the dramatic events: 'The match was heading for another draw when the referee, Eric Clay, gave Saints a try under the sticks. I couldn't believe that decision. There was an obvious knock-on but Clay ignored it. It was a bad decision for us and cost us our place at Wembley.'

So Murphy's first season in charge at the new Warrington ended in anti-climax. St Helens went on to beat Leeds 16–13 in the final to make the season even more frustrating for Murphy. Before the final he was named runner-up to Wigan's international second-row forward Bill Ashurst in the Players No. 6 player-of-the-year awards. So near again, and yet so far, on both occasions.

But for Murphy second best was never good enough. His thoughts were already focusing on the next season and on the players he would need to put himself and Warrington back at the top. He'd already made up his mind on one key player, and intended there and then to go for him.

8
Union with Aberavon

Aberavon, one of the diamonds studded in the South Wales Rugby Union belt, is a name indelibly linked with Murphy's career. With less than five minutes left for play in the 1974 Wembley final between Warrington and Featherstone Rovers the former Aberavon second-row forward, Mike Nicholas, powered his way through a bewildered Featherstone defensive barrier to score the last try of the afternoon. Those vital points made victory certain for Warrington and he was swamped in congratulations from his team-mates. Little did they know that the blond, former Union player was in considerable pain from severe injuries which were subsequently to rule him out of Great Britain's Australian tour that summer. Nicholas's try had set the seal on Murphy's boast that he would put Warrington back on top, and the Aberavon connection was firmly written into Warrington folk lore.

Mike Nicholas was one of five Rugby Union men from Aberavon who made an important contribution to Warrington's revival in the early 1970s. He adopted Warrington club and town, and after he had retired he became a successful businessman in the town where his playing days are still recalled with affection and admiration.

Two years before that famous final, back in the summer of 1972, Murphy had time to reflect on the disappointment he felt after that semi-final defeat in his first season with the club. Murphy and his family were on holiday in Cyprus at the invitation of the Warrington chairman. Murphy had just been appointed safety officer with Leonard Fairclough's, a leading northern building concern, of which Davies was also the chairman and chief executive, so this was to be a holiday mixing business with pleasure. Naturally Murphy also spent time discussing the future of Warrington and the club's need for new players.

South Africa was in Ossie Davies's sights at the time, and 'one morning at breakfast,' Murphy recalls, 'Ossie turned to me right out of the blue and asked if I would book myself on a flight to South Africa to have a look at one or two South African Rugby Union players in the Republic who might strengthen the side.' Murphy agreed to the chairman's request and booked himself on to the next flight to Johannesburg. However, the trip proved a wild goose chase. The authorities were operating severe travel restrictions on visitors and Murphy decided to fly back to Cyprus when he realized he was on a hopeless mission. Davies was philosophical about this but both men agreed that a search for new players was paramount as Murphy sought the blend which would bring an outstanding team to Warrington.

The man Murphy had at the top of his priority list was the Great Britain international, Kevin Ashcroft, his former playing partner at Leigh who had had such an outstanding game in the Cup final victory over Leeds in 1971.

'Kevin was the ideal type of player for Warrington,' recalls Murphy. 'I rated him the best hooker in the game at that time and was determined to bring him to Wilderspool. He proved me right. He was a very good player for us.' Murphy adds: 'I couldn't believe it when Leigh let him go. I'd already signed Dave Chisnall and Geoff Clarkson from them. Now I had another top player in Ashcroft. It took the heart out of the Leigh team, letting those three come to Warrington.'

Ashcroft made his debut for Murphy's team in the pre-season curtain-raiser against Wigan at Wilderspool in August 1972. It was the charity game for the Locker Cup and Wigan won comfortably despite the money Warrington had spent on new players. The home fans were not amused; neither was Murphy, who admitted his pack was 'a shambles'. But he felt inwardly that he had the nucleus of a good team and was on the right path.

Murphy was out of the team at the start of the 1972–73 season, with his old elbow injury troubling him again. But within a month he was to get an unexpected boost. The Aberavon–Warrington link had already been forged when Murphy signed the centre, Frank Reynolds, from South Wales. 'He was a good team man,' recalls Murphy. 'Frankie wasn't a big-name player but he did a good job for me.' But then Reynolds suffered an internal injury after only a handful of games and was sidelined for several matches.

The second Murphy signing from Aberavon was already in the north-west. Bobby Wonbon arrived at Wilderspool from St Helens for a modest fee of £2,500 and was to prove a bargain buy. Dennis Maddock, Warrington's scout in South Wales, was particularly pleased with the Wonbon signing. Maddock had played Rugby League a couple of times in Neath, soon after the end of the second world war, during an abortive attempt to set up the League game in South Wales. He had recommended Wonbon to Warrington's directors while Murphy was still at Leigh but much to his regret the old Warrington board rejected his recommendation and Wonbon went to St Helens instead.

Maddock says: 'Wonbon was a big, effective forward with Aberavon and I wanted Warrington to sign him. At that time a Warrington director, George Roughley, decided he'd check on the player and went against my recommendation. They apparently didn't rate him so he went to Saints instead.' Murphy had no hesitation in signing the big forward who went on to play another crucial role in Warrington's successful Challenge Cup season of 1974.

So Reynolds and Wonbon were now on the books, though the injury jinx struck again when Wonbon was sidelined after suffering knee ligament damage in his early days at Warrington. However, it was Murphy's next two signings from South Wales Rugby Union which were to prove so vital in rebuilding the team. The Aberavon winger, Dennis Curling, had already agreed to change codes and was Warrington-bound. His Aberavon colleague and friend, Clive Jones, a second-row forward, offered to drive Curling north for company. Jones also had in mind changing codes but during the journey it was no more than a thought.

When the two men arrived in Warrington Jones took Murphy by surprise by asking for a trial: 'I saw him in action just the once and signed him,' says Murphy. 'I saw enough to convince me that he would do a good job for me and be an invaluable squad man. That's the way it turned out.'

Unknown to Murphy yet another Aberavon player was pondering on the signings of Curling and Jones: their Aberavon club mate, Mike Nicholas. During that late summer of 1972 Nicholas had also journeyed north from his native Wales. He passed miles to the east of Warrington on his way to Scotland to play in the annual Border Sevens tournament. Nicholas had been selected to play for Public School Wanderers, a team traditionally made up of guest players, which had been specially invited to take part in the tournament. 'We were a good side and won the tournament that year. It was PSW's first win in about thirty years, and everyone connected with the Wanderers team was delighted.'

Public School Wanderers and friends celebrated the Sevens victory in enthusiastic style: 'I was a little hung over,' confesses Nicholas, but the hangover was to give him a thin excuse for breaking his journey home to Wales and calling in at Warrington. 'I made up my mind to call in at Warrington and take in a game. I watched the local derby against Wigan which Warrington won comfortably enough.'

Murphy liked the straight-talking, albeit abrupt, style of Nicholas from the word go. 'Nicholas stopped off on his way home to Wales and asked me for a trial. It was one of the best things that ever happened to Warrington. 'Klunk' was a great competitor and as hard as iron. Ask anyone who played against him. I should know: I played with him and that could be nerve-wracking. Mike was a superb signing in every sense,' says Murphy. He recalls his first conversation with Nicholas: 'He said to me, "I understand you've signed Curling and Jones. If they're good enough so am I. Give me a trial and I'll prove it." ' For Murphy there was nothing to lose in acceding to such a challenge. He promptly invited Nicholas to put his talents where his mouth was and gave him a trial in the Warrington 'A' team's next match against Barrow. Nicholas's performance convinced Murphy he was as good as his earlier boast and a fifth Aberavon player was now on Murphy's books.

From the moment the starting gun was fired on his career in the professional game, Nicholas was never far from the headlines or the action, particularly the action. Ironically, his debut was against the same Barrow club the following month, October 1972, when Warrington thrashed the Cumbrians 55–17. Nicholas confirmed in that game that he had the courage and ability to compete at the highest level although it was a fierce encounter for him: 'I was injured in my debut match and missed the next three games with knee ligament trouble,' he recalls glumly. Meanwhile Nicholas's family and friends in Aberavon were still reeling from the shock of him going north to play in the Border Sevens and returning home a fully fledged League player.

During the next few seasons, Nicholas was to become one of the most interesting and at times outrageous characters in the game. Stories of incidents concerning him and his time under Murphy at Warrington have spiced countless after-dinner speeches and pinned back ears in pubs and clubs wherever rugby is played.

The two men had an enduring respect for each other: 'Murph had everything. He was the best in the world,' says Nicholas. 'He was a terrific competitor and a man who led you by example. He could make ordinary players look very good ones and good players look brilliant. He was also a fantastic judge of a player's ability and could get the best out of anyone. Part of Murph's genius was his unpredictability on the field. He was quick as lightning, could pass expertly, kick with precision and was fierce in the tackle. He had courage and power.

'And I'll tell you this,' adds Nicholas in his lyrical native tongue, 'Murph could blast you with the best. He had a scathing wit and was a satirist in his own right. He also had the knack of manipulating the press which proved a big psychological advantage when dealing with players. I have always admired the great Irish racing trainer, Vincent O'Brien, who is the best in his business. Murph knew his players like O'Brien knew his horses. They are both masters with fantastic judgement.'

If the Nicholas accolades appear to give a hint that Nicholas is disingenuous, he quickly dispels any such thoughts: 'I had many stand-up rows and confrontations with Murph. But if you fell out with him it never affected his team selection. No matter how strongly you disagreed with him he was always fair-minded. He never let a good argument affect his team. If you played well you were picked to play, no matter what had been said. I admired him for that.'

Nicholas was rarely in danger of losing his place. If Murphy hinted he might be thinking of dropping his best players it was usually to spur them to greater effort. They each knew his philosophy: 'There are no automatic first-team players. You have to prove your worth to me and I'll pick you.'

1 Murphy signed for St Helens on his sixteenth birthday and was soon to show the skills which were to make him a legend in his lifetime.

2 In his early days with Great Britain, Murphy's 'minder' was 'Vinty' Karalius, the 'wild bull of the pampas'. The two of them are shown during a Great Britain training session with the late Bill Fallowfield, the former secretary of the Rugby Football League.

3 *(Above)* The St Helens team at the beginning of the 1957–58 season, Murphy's first full season with the club. The St Helens team that day was, *back row, left to right:* Dennis Karalius, Llewellyn, Terry, Johnson, Forshaw, Delves and Vince Karalius; *front row, left to right:* Alex Murphy, Finnan, McIntyre, Prescott (captain), Moses and Rhodes.

4 *(Below)* The St Helens team at the end of the 1958–59 season found Murphy already a veteran of a tour of Australia and New Zealand yet still only twenty. The St Helens team that day was, *back row, left to right:* Vince Karalius, Terry, Van Vollenhoven, Prinsloo, Fearis, Bowden, Briggs, and Huddart; *front row, left to right:* Dennis Karalius, Moses, Greenall (captain), Alex Murphy and Howard.

5 Aircraftman Murphy samples a glass of milk during his National Service days at RAF Haydock, near St Helens.

6 Murphy resumed playing with Leigh after his controversial break with St Helens which temporarily ended his playing career.

7 *(Above)* Nearly 60,000 people, half the town's population, turned out to welcome home the Saints after their 21–2 Challenge Cup final victory over Wigan in May 1966. Here Murphy holds the cup with the South African Len Killeen who had won the Lance Todd Trophy at Wembley on the Saturday.

8 *(Below)* Murphy tackles an opponent in a flurry of arms and legs as his St Helens team-mate Tom Van Vollenhoven closes in to help.

9 Alex plants a victory kiss on the cheek of his wife, Alice, as the pair hold the Challenge Cup following Leigh's triumph over the favourites, Leeds, in the 1971 final.

10 Murphy took to the sands at Southport to prepare his Warrington squad for the Challenge Cup final against Featherstone Rovers in May 1974. An exhausted Kevin Ashcroft takes a breather as Murphy points the way to victory.

11 *(Above)* Mike 'Klunk' Nicholas, the great signing Murphy made from Aberavon Rugby Union in 1973, leaps into the arms of David Chisnall, who played with Murphy at Leigh and Warrington and is now his right-hand man at St Helens, in celebration of Warrington's 24–9 victory over Featherstone Rovers in the final of the 1974 Challenge Cup. Murphy and the Warrington substitute, Bobby Wonbon, join the dance.

12 *(Below)* Murphy holds aloft the Challenge Cup after Warrington's 1974 triumph over Featherstone Rovers by 24–9.

13 Tension shows on the faces of Murphy and his assistant, Dave Chisnall (on Murphy's right), as they see the Challenge Cup slipping from their grasp against Halifax in the 1987 final when the Yorkshire side won a tremendous game 19–18.

14 The mud-spattered St Helens team hold up the John Player Special Trophy in their dressing-room after their great win over Leeds by 15–14 in the 1988 final.

15 St Helens's great but narrow victory over Leeds by 15–14 in the final of the John Player Special Trophy in January 1988 brought Murphy his first cup final win as coach of St Helens, and the club's first-ever victory in the final of the John Player competition. Here Murphy shows his relief as the hooter sounds.

9
Boxing Day Brawl

Murphy was looking forward eagerly to his second season in charge at Wilderspool. Defeat by Warrington's old rivals, Wigan, in the Locker Cup charity game in August was disappointing but Murphy was unperturbed. Kevin Ashcroft, recently signed from Leigh, had made a promising debut in that game and Murphy knew that his players would need time to settle in before getting to know each other's style of play. But he was immediately confronted by other problems.

Warrington's prop-forward, Dave Chisnall, was sent off in the last minute of the opening game of the season against Hull at Wilderspool, which was all the more irritating to Murphy because Warrington were in total command of the game and had already secured certain victory before Chisnall got his marching orders. And in the following league defeat by St Helens, his scrum-half, Parry Gordon, was also sent off and both players missed a game through suspension.

Warrington's troubles continued as they fell at the first hurdle of the Lancashire Cup; then Parry Gordon asked for a transfer. Gordon was happier about his future at the club after a personal interview with the chairman but Murphy knew he had to act quickly to pull things together on the field of play.

However, with the arrival of Mike Nicholas from Aberavon in September, Warrington's fortunes began to change and the team, now beginning to look a pretty formidable unit, settled into a winning pattern. Indeed, by mid-October, after beating Rochdale Hornets, Warrington went to the top of the table and the Murphy magic had started to work its spell again.

Approaching Christmas, Warrington were enjoying a long unbeaten run in the league and it nurtured the belief throughout the squad that this could be their year for trophies. Murphy realized that his toughest game of the season was likely to be on Boxing Day when his old club Leigh were due at Wilderspool. He knew that Leigh would be fired up under their new coach, Les Pearce, and that the pre-match publicity would fuel the old arguments and controversy that had surrounded his departure twenty months before.

Long before the Boxing Day game the battle-lines had been drawn. After the match Murphy commented: 'I think the Leigh players wanted to prove a point to their fans and to me.' Leigh certainly proved one point – or rather took one. The 6–6 scoreline was the first league point Warrington had dropped in a string of winning games at the end of 1972. The biggest crowd of the season – nearly 10,000 – packed into Wilderspool for the game on that cold December night. If they expected fireworks they were not disappointed. The ferocity of the early tackling from both sides raised the temperature.

In fact, Murphy remembers little of the encounter. He was knocked to the ground by a bone-crunching tackle just before half-time and left the field semi-conscious on a stretcher. Then his team-mate, Brian Brady, limped off as the rough stuff crept in. There was no love lost on either side, as Mike Nicholas remembers: 'The incident involving Murph really started it. Then Leigh's Tony Barrow flattened Dave Chisnall. Tony's brother Frank decided to join in and I had a go at him.' It became a free-for-all with fists flying all over the place. Then both Nicholas and Tony Barrow were given their marching orders by the Oldham referee, Sam Shepherd.

The New Year was to continue in similar fashion with no

shortage of clubs trying to knock Murphy's team out of its stride. At the end of January 1973, Warrington went to Thrum Hall in Yorkshire for the game against Halifax. It was the first round of the Challenge Cup and Halifax were a team renowned for their tough defence and hard tackling. The fans on both sides waited eagerly for the confrontation. Just before half-time Murphy was kicked on the head and left the field with blood pouring from a wound which needed stitching in the dressing-room. Then he returned to lead his team to a narrow 7–4 victory, but repercussions were to follow.

Warrington were reported to the league for tactics which were described by the Yorkshire club as 'intimidation'. The charged amused Murphy at the time: 'I couldn't believe we were being accused of intimidation. After all I was the one who was kicked on the head and had to leave the field for medical treatment,' he points out. But Murphy accepted, as he had done throughout his career, that he was a marked man. He adds: 'I was in a "no win" situation most of the time. If I got knocked down the opposing fans usually clapped as if their team had scored a try. If I knocked the opposition down the fans would boo me just as loudly. I really couldn't win. And, remember, it was me who was stretchered off at Halifax.'

Despite the toughness of the games, Warrington continued their unbeaten sequence in the championship as the Challenge Cup second-round tie with Widnes approached. Anticipation ran high, with Murphy confident that his team would prove too efficient in every department for the men from Naughton Park. The correctness of his pre-match judgement was endorsed when Warrington ran out comfortable winners by 20–8.

Wilderspool was now buzzing with excitement. The home supporters believed that the disappointments of the previous season, when St Helens knocked them out of the Challenge Cup at the final hurdle, would soon vanish. Murphy's players too had that extra zip in training sessions that comes with the conviction that they now had sufficient strength in depth to take on and beat the best teams in the game. But again they were to be disappointed. Murphy left his team behind for the game with Rochdale Hornets at the end of February so that he could go on a 'spying mission' to Featherstone Rovers, Warrington's opponents in the quarter-finals of the Challenge Cup. But while Murphy was planning the downfall of the Yorkshiremen, his Warrington team were slumping to their first home defeat of the season against Hornets. That set-back not only ended Warrington's long unbeaten run, it also derailed their Cup train and the club crashed out of the Challenge Cup 14–18 to Featherstone Rovers, the eventual winners at Wembley, the following week. The Warrington fans were incredulous; Murphy was stunned.

However, Warrington bounced back from their week of heartache with a rousing victory over Huyton and then completed the double over Oldham at Watersheddings to go joint top of the championship table with Leeds. They were to be further consoled from an unlikely source. Featherstone Rovers, who had knocked Warrington out of the Cup, clinched the league leader's title for Warrington by beating Leeds in the league despite Featherstone's own preoccupation with Wembley. It was an unexpected win for Featherstone. Most pundits had felt that with the Cup final on their minds they would ease up in the league. But they were clearly under orders to keep the momentum going to earn their places at Wembley. It was an attitude that Murphy understood and admired for he had always insisted that his players should not ease up when they were involved in big cup matches: 'You owe it to your spekkies to give a hundred per cent in every game. They help to pay your wages and anything less than maximum effort would be cheating them.'

More important for Warrington, the Featherstone win over Leeds had eased the pressure of the two Easter games to come. Warrington now knew that no matter what happened in those matches, against Widnes and Leigh, the league leader's title was theirs.

The League Leader's Trophy was duly displayed in the Warrington board-room as Murphy's second season in charge now reached its climax with the championship play-offs. Warrington beat Wigan in the first round and then went on to overpower Rochdale Hornets in the second to ease themselves into the semi-finals. Once again, however, Warrington were to be disappointed, losing to Dewsbury in the semi-final at Wilderspool. It was a hard-fought game with the Yorkshiremen nosing in front 12–7 and eventually going on to win the championship.

Murphy felt that particular disappointment as deeply as the fans. Despite winning the League Leader's Trophy, it seemed to him that defeat in the play-offs had undone much of the hard work of two seasons. Warrington were still not quite there. 'I knew the team needed extra quality in a couple of key positions. If I could find the right players to slot in I was sure we could be a match for anyone,' was Murphy's belief as he vowed that his third season at Wilderspool would be the one to make up for the previous disappointments and near misses.

10
Crossroads for Murphy

Rugby Union's heartland in South Wales provided Warrington with players who gave the team strength, skill and stability during the early part of Murphy's reign at Wilderspool. The Aberavon five – Mike Nicholas, Frank Reynolds, Dennis Curling, Clive Jones and Bobby Wonbon – made a vital contribution to Warrington's success story in the 1970s and it was to be another Welshman of high calibre whose arrival helped to launch the 1973–74 season, the most successful in the club's history.

John Bevan, of Wales, the British Lions and Cardiff, took Warrington by storm. 'We all know they can sing in Wales,' says Murphy, 'but I can tell you this fella Bevan made sweet music for us at Warrington.' Bevan had established his Union reputation with club and country throughout the rugby world before heading north from his native valleys for a new career in Rugby League. Murphy was ecstatic when Bevan agreed to change codes. He recognized that Bevan's innate world-class ability, allied to a big-match temperament, would produce the extra points needed to turn Warrington from the 'nearly men' into an outstanding team.

From the moment Bevan scored a try on his debut in the victory over Castleford in September 1973, the Wilderspool fans needed no more convincing that they had someone very special in their team. 'When he first joined us, John Bevan was a very good player. Once he'd grasped the League game he became a brilliant player,' says Murphy now. Following in the footsteps of the great Brian Bevan, the club's former international hero, John Bevan had the surname to endear him to everyone at Warrington. His skill, pace and try-scoring feats did the rest and he was soon the crowd's favourite.

One aspect of Bevan immediately impressed the perfectionist in Murphy: 'He was a fanatical trainer, a great individualist and also a good team man. I couldn't have asked for more from John. He was a smashing lad all round.' And he never let Murphy down. But even the superb Bevan felt Murphy's wrath, and despite his wizardry the Warrington coach was quick to tell him there was one part of his play he wouldn't tolerate.

'John started a craze which today's soccer players have followed. He used to punch the air with one arm in a victory salute before scoring a try. I warned him I didn't like the habit. It was unprofessional and the rest of the team started copying him. It became a craze throughout the club and I could see it causing us problems. I took John to one side and warned him that if he ever dropped the ball as he was going over the try-line and punching the air in his victory salute, I'd leave him out of the team. And I told the rest of the lads that anyone copying the habit would get the same treatment.'

Murphy's ban on 'air punching', as he called it, before a try was scored, quickly stamped out the habit. 'Some of the players couldn't catch the ball properly, never mind run with it in one hand, while they were punching the air with the other. But John was a superb showman and such a likable lad it was difficult to tell him off. So I threatened their pay packets and it did the trick.'

Warrington had been so keen to sign John Bevan that Murphy went personally with Ossie Davies to the player's home. Murphy recalls the journey: 'John lived in a little terrace row with the house overlooking a huge tip like a small mountain. When we got there John's father told us he used it for his training sessions. He apparently ran up and down the slopes. Believe me, a mountain goat would have had a job running up and down that tip.'

But that journey to Bevan's home was an important first step in writing a new chapter in Warrington's history. 'John had just come back from a Lions tour,' says Murphy, 'and I was delighted when he agreed to join us. And we did well for each other, didn't we? John finished up having a benefit at Warrington, and only a handful of players achieve that. To earn a benefit you have to prove yourself over ten years, and that is just how confident a player John became.'

Bevan's Warrington career got off on the wrong foot. After scoring a try on his debut against Castleford, he left the field injured before half-time. Murphy followed him, sent off for fighting though he insists he wasn't angered by the injury to Bevan. That game had an immediate effect on Bevan. He realized there would be no easy money in the league and that pay packets would have to be earned the hard way. What he didn't realize then was that his first season in Rugby League would prove sensational for him and his new club.

Shortly after Bevan's arrival, Murphy sensed a slackening off in the attitude of his players. He responded to a poor team display after a defeat by Featherstone Rovers by banning his players from using the games facilities at the club's leisure centre. The leisure and sports complex at Wilderspool was the envy of many clubs and a favourite meeting point for the players after training sessions.

'Some players were staying in the centre longer than I felt they should and it seemed to me it was affecting their play. I was determined we were not going to suffer on the field because of it,' says Murphy. 'There were other things they should have had on their minds, like rugby, which is what they were being paid for at Warrington. So I put the leisure centre out of bounds.'

Murphy also had other things on his mind: the team had lost form and the first round of a new sponsored competition was approaching – the Captain Morgan Trophy, dubbed the 'rum trophy'. It was to be in the semi-final against Leeds that a serious injury nearly ended Murphy's playing career.

Murphy knew that if Warrington could reach the final, and win the trophy, it would bring in much-needed cash to help strengthen his squad. His team took the field in peak condition, with the players sharing his conviction that they would beat Leeds. The match then followed Murphy's expectations, a hard battle for the ascendency with much tough tackling. The Leeds supporters, he recalls, became increasingly irritated by their team's inability to gain the initiative over a Warrington team which was still something of an unknown quantity and had yet to prove itself in major competitions. Moreover, Murphy's inspirational leadership had begun to tell. His precision-kicking was pushing the Leeds team back towards their own 25-yard line every time they threatened the Warrington defences. It was a tactic which increased the frustration of the opposition and Murphy knew they were losing their grip on the game.

But Murphy was to pay a severe penalty for his brilliance, as he recounts: 'I kicked the ball deep into the Leeds half as they came at us and was going at full speed after it. I remember their international hooker, Tony Fisher, closing in to intercept. Suddenly I was stopped dead in my tracks and crashed to the ground. From then on it's all a blur.' Fisher's tackle left Murphy flat on his back, barely conscious. 'I knew my jaw had been broken,' recalls Murphy, 'because I felt a "popping" sensation high up on the side of my face as the tackle was made.'

The referee incensed the Warrington fans by awarding them only a penalty despite their howls of protest and demands that Fisher should be sent off. Meanwhile Murphy was in the dressing-room, slowly regaining his senses. As the numbness stiffened one side of his face, he knew he had a serious injury. 'I was told later that a touch-judge had informed the referee that I must have been all right because he saw me "yapping" in the Leeds board-room after the game. What the touch-judge didn't know was that the break was high up on my jaw which meant I could speak although it was very painful.'

The incident served to illustrate how Murphy's reputation had made him a marked man, with some officials unwilling to accept that he wasn't always trying to 'con' them. Any doubts that he was play-acting during the Fisher incident at Leeds were swept away when Murphy entered Liverpool Infirmary and underwent a three-and-a-half hour operation on his shattered jaw. Murphy vowed that he wouldn't allow the injury to end his career. He was advised that it might be the right time to hang up his boots, but he wouldn't listen. Mike Nicholas was stunned at the extent of the injury. 'None of the lads realized Murph had been so badly hurt until we found out he was in hospital. He was such a showman you couldn't tell how badly hurt he was.'

Warrington's delight at reaching the Captain Morgan final was tempered with the knowledge that Murphy would need a long time to recover from his broken jaw. And when the team was beaten at home by their great rivals, Wigan, on New Year's Day 1974 there was little to suggest that Warrington had already reached the launching-pad for a spectacular end to their season.

Though Warrington were through to the quarter-final of one sponsored competition, the Players No. 6 Trophy, and the final of another, the Captain Morgan, they realized that the going would now be a good deal tougher without Murphy's great qualities of leadership on the field. Rumours were circulating that Murphy would now hang up his boots; indeed he was being urged to do that. But his personal courage and determination to play again never faltered.

Dewsbury were brushed aside in the Players No. 6 quarter-final and St Helens were beaten in the semi-final in January as Warrington reached their second sponsored competition final. Then they beat Featherstone Rovers to win the Captain Morgan Trophy. It was Murphy's first success for the club in a knock-out competition and the first for its new management team of Davies and Pitchford, who had put faith in him when they brought him to the club nearly three years before.

11

Twin Towers

Warrington's Captain Morgan Trophy win gave them a unique success, for the sponsors withdrew their support after the first year, leaving the club the only winners of the competition. It was ironic that Warrington's hero in the final was their goal-kicking full-back, Derek Whitehead. With defences in command only four points were scored throughout the match, all from the boot of Whitehead, whose two superbly struck penalty-goals in the opening minutes clinched a 4–0 victory over Featherstone Rovers. Whitehead was making amends for what had happened nearly two years earlier – in April 1972 – when Warrington had lost to St Helens in the semi-final of the Challenge Cup after a replay.

The win did more than just give the new management team its first knock-out cup success; it also gave the club immense confidence at all levels and brought in the hard cash which allowed Murphy to buy his final piece in the team jig-saw. While his players debated what they would be doing with their record bonus from the sponsored competition, Murphy had already decided what the club would be doing with the £3,000 winner's cheque – and he didn't intend it should be paid into the club's bank account.

For some weeks he'd nurtured the idea of signing the loose forward, Barry Philbin, from Swinton. Philbin's brother Mike was already a key player at Warrington and Murphy wanted both men in his team. He went to his bosses, Davies and Pitchford, within minutes of the Captain Morgan triumph and urged them to use the £3,000 to buy Barry Philbin. The two directors could do little but stand by their word that Murphy would have full control over the buying and selling of players, and agreed to his request. Swinton's chairman, Jack Bateman, insisted that no deal should be signed until the money was in the Swinton bank account. Within forty-eight hours of the Captain Morgan win Swinton had the money and Warrington had a new loose forward. The key to Warrington's Wembley success had been cut.

Barry Philbin was bewildered by the speed of events which took him from Station Road, Swinton, to Wilderspool. But at Warrington Philbin's signing provided the opening of a sensational chapter of success. Brian Pitchford recalls the events: 'We could tell how much AJ wanted to sign Barry Philbin when he asked us to pay out the Captain Morgan cheque straightaway to Swinton. And I remember Philbin becoming a key player for us in that season's success story. He was AJ's choice and we let him sign him. How Barry was ignored by the selectors for that summer's Great Britain tour I will never understand. He was an outstanding player for us at Warrington.'

To underline Pitchford's assessment, the records show that Philbin made his Warrington debut in the first round of the Challenge Cup in February 1974 – a week after signing for the club. From that game on, bonuses were being earned by Philbin and his new team-mates for the rest of the season. Warrington's Cup train built up its head of steam with a convincing Challenge Cup first-round win over Huddersfield by 34–4 to put the club on line for Wembley. The following week brought another major success when they beat Rochdale Hornets 27–16 in the Players No. 6 final, their second victory in a sponsored competition. In that game Warrington's hooker, Kevin Ashcroft, the player Murphy had brought from his former club Leigh, was named man-of-the-match, the first Lancashire winner in the competition to date. Players and supporters alike at Wilderspool couldn't wait for the Challenge Cup second-round visit of Huyton, who put up only token resistance against a Warrington team fired up through its twin successes in the sponsored competitions and with the Wembley 'roar' growing louder with each win.

With Huyton brushed aside by 21–6, the scene was set for the Challenge Cup quarter-finals and for Warrington a match against Wigan at Central Park, in early March 1974. The clubs had met only three times in the Challenge Cup in recent history, and Wigan had won each time. Murphy realized that Wigan would start favourites and home advantage would give them the edge. He had to bring his players to the peak of condition for a match in which fitness could swing the balance between two very good sides. So the Wilderspool training sessions left the Warrington players tired, drained, and aching as they prepared for the Cup battle with the old enemy.

Murphy impressed on his players that the best way to prepare for the Wigan clash was to keep their momentum going in the intervening league games. The players responded with a splendid win over Dewsbury only seven days before the Challenge Cup quarter-final. That victory convinced fans of both teams that the Cup game would be a great contest and they packed into Central Park for the encounter. However, with so much at stake tempers on both sides were on a short fuse and the game was an explosive affair. Three drop-goals from Kevin Ashcroft gave Warrington the decisive edge and Murphy's men booked their semi-final ticket with a 10–6 victory that was in doubt until the final hooter.

Memories of the game are still vivid. Albert White, whom Murphy had brought from Salford to take charge of the scouting system at Wilderspool, watched the game from the Warrington bench alongside Murphy and recalls how he became embroiled in the events of the afternoon. Mike Nicholas, the man they nicknamed 'Klunk', was soon in the thick of the action. Tackling was fierce from both teams until the rule book was thrown out of the ground as Nicholas started fighting with Wigan's international forward, Eddie Cunningham, who, he believed, had punched him. Both players were sent off.

Albert White followed the players down the tunnel where they started fighting again. He tried to separate them and instantly regretted his indiscretion: 'Klunk caught me with a punch to the side of my jaw as I jumped in between them,' White remembers. Later, Nicholas sat quietly in the dressing-room looking dejected. 'Murphy said to him, "They should have bricked up the Welsh mountains to keep you inside and I would be a happier man",' White recalls. 'I wanted to laugh but I couldn't move my jaw.'

The incident appeared to be over as the atmosphere cooled down. But Murphy and White were in for another shock. White takes up the story: 'Next to the Wigan dressing-room is the communal bath used by the players. We heard noises coming from the bath area and went inside to investigate. Klunk had Cunningham by the hair and was trying to push him under the water. Murphy jumped into the bath fully clothed and tried to pull the players apart. He had to hit Klunk to make him release his grip on Cunningham. Murphy was soaking wet and took off his shoes to let the water out,' says White, who left the dressing-room to go in search of the club groundsman, Billy Mitchell. 'I asked Billy if he had a pair of gum boots I could borrow because Murphy's shoes were soaking wet. When Murphy put them on they were four sizes too big. I tried to laugh but I couldn't because of my jaw which was still swelling.' So the two men trudged back to the Wigan bench to concentrate on the rugby.

Mike Nicholas recalls the events of the afternoon philosophically: 'The game had generated intense rivalry and we launched into Wigan from the start. That was the only way to win at Central Park. I think it got through to the Wigan players that they weren't going to win. Eddie Cunningham was a very good player but got frustrated, I think. The game was at fever pitch and we started fighting after he caught me. I was a bit annoyed at being sent off. I didn't think I'd started the trouble and wanted to stay on. I was so wound up I even back-handed one of my own team-mates when I was leaving the field after being sent off.'

The victory over Wigan set up a money-spinning semi-final against Dewsbury and meant that Warrington had a chance of reaching their first Challenge Cup final for twenty years. The club's last appearance at Wembley had been in the 1954 final when a 4–4 stalemate with Halifax meant a replay in front of more than 100,000 fans at Bradford's Odsal Stadium. Then Warrington's outstanding player, scrum-half Gerry Helme, sealed an 8–4 victory near the end with an opportunist's try which earned him the man-of-the-match Lance Todd Trophy.

The week before the 1974 Challenge Cup semi-final Murphy's 'second string' thirteen won a league game at Castleford to underline Warrington's growing belief that this was going to be their year. Confidence throughout the club was now rooted in rock, providing a strength of purpose too powerful for Dewsbury to resist in the semi-finals as the 'Wire' triumphed yet again by 17–7.

Psychologically, Warrington already had the upper hand after a narrow league victory over Rovers a month before Wembley, and Murphy felt that by winning that Cup final 'rehearsal' against Featherstone his players had given themselves the cutting edge. Murphy had now fully recoved from the broken jaw he had suffered in the Captain Morgan semi-final at Leeds four months earlier. He was match fit and rarin' to go. But he was becoming increasingly concerned that his players were preoccupied with the Wembley final and sensed an air of complacency and over-confidence creeping in. He issued a stern warning to his playing staff: 'Prove yourselves to me or you'll not be at Wembley.' His words got through to the players. Mike Nicholas, in particular, was to show the spirit of determination in, for him, an unusual way. 'On the run-in to Wembley we played Widnes in the league,' he recalls. 'One of their players, Brian Hogan, had a real go at me. Normally I would have done something about it there and then. But I just whispered to him, "I'm going to the 'twin towers', boy. I'll catch up with you later."'

Apart from the Widnes game the Wembley build-up could hardly have been tougher on Warrington with the team also involved in the Championship play-offs. In the first round they beat Hull and followed up with victory over Bradford Northern, the previous season's second division champions.

Then in the semi-final they beat Wakefield Trinity, though the match ended disastrously for Murphy himself. Mid-way through the second half he was stretchered off, writhing in pain from a rib injury that was to threaten his Wembley place. The final was only six days away.

Plans for Cup final week had already been laid to bring the players to a peak of condition for the London stage. There were to be three days at Fulwood army barracks in Preston for intensive training on the assault course, and then the team would travel to their London headquarters where Murphy hoped to put finishing touches to some planned moves in the concluding work-outs. 'Murphy pulled us off the assault course on the first day,' laughs Mike Nicholas. 'He felt there was too big a risk of injury to the lads at that army camp.' Instead, Murphy turned to the Southport sands, a favourite training area, for inspiration in the days leading to the final. The Warrington squad found itself in good company if it wanted a winning omen for the legendary Grand National winner, Red Rum, was also going through its paces on the Southport sands that week and Murphy, with a fascination for horses, was delighted.

Murphy headed off any press speculation which might have had an unsettling effect on his players by naming his Wembley team at Southport, picking himself at stand-off and the long-serving Parry Gordon at scrum-half. The team sheet read: Derek Whitehead, Mike Philbin, Derek Noonan, Alan Whittle, John Bevan, Alex Murphy, Parry Gordon, David Chisnall, Kevin Ashcroft, Brian Brady, David Wright, Mike Nicholas, Barry Philbin. The two substitutes were Billy Pickup and Bob Wonbon.

The talking was over. Three days before the final Murphy

and his squad went south to their London headquarters at the Kensington Palace Hotel. They were bonded together by a single purpose – to bring the Rugby League Challenge Cup back to Warrington.

12
A Town for Alex

Murphy had climbed the Matterhorn to get himself in shape for the Cup final. Only five months earlier he had been on the operating-table at Liverpool Royal Infirmary, his rugby career hanging in the balance. He was unaware at the time just how seriously he'd been hurt by the head injury he'd suffered in that match against Leeds. Only the skill of the medical team at the Liverpool hospital had given him the chance of making a full recovery. He was told later that the blow to his upper jaw could have left him permanently incapacitated if it had caught him half an inch higher. But Murphy refused to let the knowledge make him quit the game he loved, though close friends were urging him to do so.

'Rugby League's a very hard game and you have to accept the risks and danger you face while playing,' he said philosophically. His wife, Alice, who fully understood just how hard the game could be, was shocked by the injury: 'It was a very bad break indeed. It was a very worrying time for us.' But Murphy's personal courage, physical strength and determination to play again all helped in his recovery. He repeatedly rejected suggestions that he should hang up his boots and focused his thoughts on how soon he could play again.

Though he joked with friends and players about the injury, it caused him much concern. He had been an all-action man throughout his career and had a big appetite for training. His broken jaw had pushed him into touch and he didn't like the experience one bit. However, to some extent, he had been a victim of his own reputation for 'play-acting'. Referees and touch-judges had been made sceptical by players acting hurt during the game. Murphy himself had often been accused of 'milking' injury situations to give his team an extra advantage.

But on that cold Saturday afternoon of 8 December 1973, against Leeds, one man knew instantly that his was not an Oscar-winning performance from a player feigning injury. Brian Pitchford, by now a close personal friend of Murphy off the field, realized straightaway that Murphy was badly hurt. 'When AJ fell to the ground he lost possession of the ball. I knew instantly he was hurt. I had often seen AJ play-acting but whenever that happened he always knew where the ball was. At Leeds he didn't bother where the ball had gone and just lay in obvious pain. When I saw him later, the injury to his face looked terrible. The side of his face was pushed in. I don't think any of us realized just how badly hurt he was until he went into hospital and underwent a long operation. We all admired his determination to carry on although we doubted the wisdom of it. But then AJ is a winner and doesn't give in easily.'

Murphy spent a miserable Christmas with his family and close friends at his bungalow home in Bold, a few miles from the St Helens town centre. His broken jaw was wired and immobile, leaving him with a deep sense of frustration and uneasy about his future: sidelined from the game he loved, his spirits were at a low ebb. And being unable to eat or drink properly throughout the Christmas period further exacerbated his problems.

His thoughts wandered over a distinguished career which had already brought him every honour the game could bestow. Maybe now was the time to hang up his boots as he approached his thirty-fifth birthday. It was a fleeting thought which he quickly dismissed. Quitting wasn't a word in Murphy's vocabulary. The idea of throwing in the towel was anathema to him: 'I did not want injury to end my career abruptly. I still felt I was good enough to come back.'

Then on Boxing Day 1973, his confidence was boosted by his team's victory over his former club, Leigh, and he again began to feel twinges of excitement as he thought of playing again. John Bevan destroyed Leigh with a four-try performance in that match, which won for Warrington a locally sponsored trophy of little consequence in itself but which nevertheless was the first cup win in a season which was to make the Warrington trophy-cupboard the envy of the Rugby League world.

But that match seemed a century ago as Murphy reflected on his serious rib injury with the Featherstone Rovers final only six days away. He was understandably thoroughly dejected, believing the injury would cost him a place in the team at Wembley. 'I'd agonized through the weeks when I was recovering from my broken jaw about playing again and then this happened,' he said at the time. In fact, Murphy need not have worried. He cut ball work from his training during those days, in case he should get another knock on his ribs, and with intensive daily treatment he passed himself fit on the eve of the game.

Murphy had a dedicated and experienced back-up team at Warrington. Derek (Nobby) Clarke, his number two, and Tom Grainey, the 'A' team coach, were both former players and knew the game inside out. Both men well knew the importance of building up to a big match correctly. They agreed with Murphy that it was vital to get the players physically and mentally prepared for the big day at Wembley.

Clarke was a natural athlete who had turned down the chance of trials with Lancashire as a schoolboy cricketer. He was also a keen swimmer, cyclist and rugby player. While serving in the Army he had played rugby for his regimental side against the Navy and enjoyed the experience. After completing his national service Clarke signed professional forms for Warrington in the early 1950s and stayed with the club throughout his career, spanning a quarter of a century, before easing himself out of the game to concentrate on his job with a big northern brewery. Injury had shortened his playing days and in the early 1960s he took charge of the 'A' team at Wilderspool, before Grainey joined the club from Leigh.

Clarke recalls Murphy's arrival at Warrington in a blaze of publicity after Leigh's sensational Challenge Cup win over the hot-favourites Leeds when Murphy had inspired them to their 1971 Cup success. 'When AJ joined us he asked me if I wanted to be with him and the first team or to stay with the 'A' team. I got on well with him from the start. He was a superb motivator and whenever he pulled on the club jersey the team was lifted by his presence; you could sense that. I felt confident that with AJ we could make Warrington a force again and was delighted to become his number two.'

Grainey, like Clarke, also knew Murphy well. He'd played alongside him in the Leigh team at Hilton Park: 'Murphy was an excellent judge of players and was a brilliant player himself. I remember when he was at Leigh the Australians thought he was the best player they had ever seen. And I will tell you this: in all my years in the game I've never seen a better one.'

Grainey believes that part of Murphy's genius stemmed from his unpredictability. 'He was a "spark" player. He often didn't know what to do until he got the ball in his hands. He could make openings out of nothing. If there was the slightest gap he was through it. He had pace to burn, he was so quick. When he came to Leigh from St Helens in the late 1960s we had a champion sprinter at the club. Murphy could match him over fifty yards; and remember he'd played at St Helens for ten years before he came to Hilton Park. Murph was like a great conductor of an orchestra. If he played well, we all played well. Even if he was off form for some reason or other he was still too good to be left out of the team. Mind you, if he wasn't playing because of an injury or for some other reason, he was the worst possible spectator. He was that up-tight on the bench he couldn't bear to watch the lads and used to go for a walk round the ground. He was always so keyed up on match days because he so much wanted us to win.'

Murphy's impact in just three years at Warrington had been noticed throughout the rugby-playing world. During that successful 1974 Challenge Cup run he was 'sounded out', not for the first time in his career, by an Australian club. They wanted him for a dozen games and were prepared to pay him £5,000 for his services. As Grainey recalls: 'Murphy's reputation with the Australians was sky-high.' He was still remembered as Great Britain's youngest-ever tourist down-under sixteen years earlier when his brilliance as a teenager had thrust him on to the international stage.

However, for all his pedigree, Murphy still had to fulfil his promise to Warrington that he would put the club back at the top and the 1974 Challenge Cup offered him the best chance yet to keep that promise. Derek Clarke suggested that Southport sands offered an ideal training area for the players in Cup final week. 'We'd often heard stories of players suffering cramp on the lush Wembley turf and I felt the sand dunes at Southport would be an ideal training-ground to strengthen the players' leg muscles,' recalls Clarke. Training schedules were planned in detail in order to bring the players to peak condition on the day. There were training runs along the beach and through the shallow sea water; swimming sessions were followed by sauna and turkish baths; and, the favourite with the players, soaking in a brine bath. 'When we headed for our London headquarters three days before the final everyone felt it was going to be our year,' Clarke remembers. 'We all felt in superb shape and ready to face anything.'

Murphy and his Cup final squad arrived in London at lunchtime on the Thursday. After unpacking at the Kensington Palace Hotel the players donned their training gear and headed for a training session in the adjoining Hyde Park. Cup final eve, however, was to provide a moment of pure pantomime which briefly threatened all their meticulous planning. On the Friday morning they visited Wembley Stadium to psych themselves up for the big game. 'The Wembley ground staff were working on the surface of the pitch and couldn't believe their eyes at what was to follow,' recalls Clarke. 'Our lads ran up the steps leading to the Royal Box as if they had won the cup and one of them held an imaginary trophy aloft in a victory salute. It was a mock ceremony of what they felt would happen the next day. That is how confident they all were. The team spirit was two hundred and one per cent. I believe we would have beaten anyone in the final, no matter who we had played,' Clarke insists.

Back at the hotel the players changed again into their rugby gear for another training session in Hyde Park. A moment of pure theatre was about to begin.

Patrolling the park were several uniformed attendants with the French sentry's cry of *qui vive* clearly on their minds. The afternoon's training was in full swing with the Warrington squad involved in a 'tick and pass' session near the Albert Memorial. The session was designed to sharpen reflexes. If a player dropped the ball or gave a forward pass during the exercise he had to run up and down the memorial steps and do half a dozen press-ups as a 'punishment'.

Brian Pitchford, accompanied by his wife Carol, had left the hotel for a stroll in the park and decided it would be a good idea to watch the players going through their routines. Warrington's heavyweight kit and baggage man, affectionately known as Ockher, saw the couple and offered them deck-chairs so that they could watch in comfort. It was at that moment that one of the uniformed park attendants felt duty bound to intervene.

'Can't you read?' the irate attendant bawled at Pitchford.

'Of course I can,' replied Pitchford politely thinking at the time that the man closely resembled the television funny man, Derek Guyler. 'And can that lot?' the park official snapped back, wagging his finger towards the players training nearby. 'I believe they can,' confirmed Pitchford. Realizing there was a misunderstanding, and in an attempt to cool the situation, Pitchford told the park official that 'that lot' was in fact Warrington Rugby League team training for the following day's Challenge Cup final at Wembley.

The explanation fell on deaf ears as the implacable official pointed angrily at a sign and demanded another urgent answer from Pitchford. 'What does that say?' 'Keep off the grass,' responded Pitchford. The reply was red rag to a bull. 'What are you doing sitting on the grass then?' fumed the attendant. 'Watching them,' Pitchford answered calmly, indicating the Warrington players and Murphy going through their training routines.

Pitchford's polite though tongue-in-cheek dialogue with the official alas went unnoticed. 'They're the next lot I'm going to tackle,' he shouted back. At this point Warrington's burly baggage man, Ockher, strolled over to the Pitchfords, having heard the commotion. Pitchford smiles as he recalls the bizarre event which followed: 'Ockher asked me if the park man was troubling me. And he offered to throw the poor man over the bushes if he was. I said, "Don't kill the poor chap, he's only doing his job."'

Unfortunately, the obvious humour of the discussion between the Warrington men hadn't penetrated the serious mood of the official. So, to appease him, the Warrington party moved to another spot in the park. Meanwhile the attendant had followed the players and confronted Derek Clarke who was conducting the 'tick and pass' session. 'Get this lot off here. No one is allowed on the grass,' he growled at Clarke. 'You'd better tell the manager,' Clarke replied, pointing to Murphy. Murphy was furious at the interruption. 'What is the trouble, BJ?' he asked his director-boss Pitchford, who called back, 'The park attendant's insisting we all keep off the grass.'

Murphy glared at the official: 'Look at that lot,' he said, pointing to his players. 'Some of the biggest, fittest and toughest men in Rugby League – and you're going to throw them off the grass?' Attempts to explain that Warrington had permission to use the park for their Wembley training left the attendant unimpressed. Pitchford recalls how the interlude reached its farcical conclusion: 'The official pulled out his walkie-talkie radio and shouted, "Hello, park to office. Can you hear me? I have a bunch of yobbos playing rugby in the park and they won't move. They tell me they are playing at Wimbledon tomorrow." He had obviously misheard me when I said Wembley. But after a pause he was quickly called back to his office.' Murphy and the players saw the funnier side of the incident later when they returned to the hotel. It provided light relief and was a relaxing diversion to the evening's after-dinner conversations as tension mounted. Murphy summed up the affair: 'I don't think the park man was a rugby fan.'

The Warrington players had little time to dwell on the big game on Cup final eve. Murphy and his back-room staff had decided to keep them occupied by having a night out at the pictures. The film they chose was the recently released *Towering Inferno* which tells what happens when fire rages through the world's tallest building and people panic as they become trapped by the flames. 'It was supposed to take our minds off the following day's Cup final but I thought it was absolutely terrifying,' says Derek Clarke. 'The lads seemed to take it in their stride and it didn't seem to have any effect on Murphy. But it certainly got its message through to me.'

Ironically, Richard Chamberlain, one of the stars of the film, was also staying at the same hotel as the Warrington team. But Chamberlain's presence provided little comfort for Clarke who feared the nightmare could become a reality. 'The Kensington Palace Hotel is a tall building, and I couldn't help thinking what would happen if fire broke out while we were asleep. The fire precautions at the hotel were absolutely first-class but after watching that film I checked all the fire-exit doors, fire-escapes and read the fire-drill instructions before going to sleep.'

Meanwhile, some of the players were playing cards in one of the rooms. But they were more bothered by the noise outside the hotel. Warrington's international hooker, Kevin Ashcroft, takes up the story: 'Some Featherstone spekkies were outside making as much noise as they could, obviously thinking we were asleep. A couple of lads got buckets of water, opened windows and tried to empty the buckets over the heads of the rowdies. Unfortunately at that moment a man came out of the hotel to get into a Rolls-Royce and was drenched. It was embarrassing to say the least. I can tell you we all went to bed very quickly indeed.'

On Saturday morning, with the big game now only hours

away, Murphy took his squad into Hyde Park for one more loosening-up session. 'We played soccer with a rugby ball,' remembers Clarke. 'It was a good laugh, as you can imagine, and helped relax everyone. The atmosphere was great. I don't think anyone would have beaten us on the day.'

Brian Pitchford recalls the tension mounting on Cup-final morning at the hotel. 'Murph was like a cat on hot bricks. He's always up-tight before a big game and this was the biggest game we'd faced at Warrington since AJ took over nearly three years earlier. We all knew he would be like that, and kept out of his way.'

There was, of course, little left to say. The training, swimming, running, sweating and fine tuning of the week was about to undergo a thorough examination by Featherstone Rovers. Murphy believed no more could have been done to prepare his team for battle. The management and staff at the Kensington Palace Hotel joined with the fans in clapping and cheering the players as they boarded the coach for the journey to Wembley, a handshake, an autograph, a slap on the back and a word of encouragement being the final acts in the tribal ritual as the team moved out.

'We believed we were as good as Featherstone in every position and, with Murphy's leadership, we had the edge,' commented Pitchford afterwards. 'We all recognized that Featherstone had many outstanding players, such as Keith Bridges and Steve Nash, but we felt it was going to be our day.'

Murphy's *bête noir* throughout his career has been players who dress too casually on the way to a big game. 'He's never been one for tolerating sloppy appearances,' remembers Pitchford. 'The lads really looked the part on the coach travelling to Wembley in their club blazers and ties. They looked immaculate. That's the way AJ liked things to be.'

Pitchford vividly recalls a poignant moment as the Warrington team coach approached the 'twin towers'. 'The players had made a recording of the club's song *Primrose and Blue*. As we moved along Wembley Way, Murphy asked the lads to open the windows and sing the club song so our own spekkies walking to the stadium would hear and join in. It was a great moment for us all.'

The final itself was a bruising affair. Mike Nicholas recalls Murphy making a fierce early tackle on Featherstone's three-quarter, David Hartley: 'It was a real crunching tackle and set the tone from the start,' says Nicholas. Featherstone, too, had their tacticians. Murphy recalls their international scrum-half, Steve Nash, trying to goad him: 'I heard Steve shout to his big forwards to run at the "old man", meaning me. He wanted to win like we did. But they came unstuck. We were too good for them on the day.' Warrington's winning score of 24–9 underlined Murphy's view, which was emphasized when their full-back, Derek Whitehead, took the Lance Todd Trophy as man-of-the-match after kicking his way to a 14-point tally. And yet the first half of the final had gone against Warrington's hopes.

The Featherstone full-back, Harold Box, opened the scoring with a penalty which his opposite number, Derek Whitehead, equalized within minutes. Warrington nosed in front with another Whitehead penalty but Box returned the compliment. Then two more penalties from Whitehead appeared to give Warrington the initiative with an 8–4 lead.

Then concern spread through the Warrington camp as the inspirational Murphy limped from the field holding sore ribs and nursing a groin strain. With Murphy off the field, Rovers' stand-off and skipper, John Newlove, broke through the Warrington defence and dived for the line, holding off a despairing challenge from Mike Nicholas. Box converted the try and the half-time score showed Featherstone back in front 9–8 and Warrington facing the prospect of a full second half without Murphy.

Murphy, who has a secret dread of needles, was given five pain-killing injections to get him back on to the field and into the action. 'I was more worried about the needles than I was about the big Featherstone forwards,' he admitted later. Tom Grainey, sitting on the Warrington bench, remembers that Murphy felt at one stage that he couldn't carry on. 'We pleaded with him to stay on. He was playing so well. If he'd come off I think it would have disrupted everything and cost us the Cup.'

Murphy's return lifted Warrington and they soon regained the lead. Kevin Ashcroft raced on to a pass from Derek Noonan and powered over the Featherstone line for a try converted by Whitehead. Warrington now led 13–9 and had one hand firmly on the Cup within five minutes of the re-start. Murphy seized on the situation and arrowed two superb drop-goals to sap the morale of the Yorkshiremen and push his team further ahead. The sight of the injured Murphy still dictating affairs frustrated Rovers even more and the match boiled over into a brawl. Several players joined in – Warrington's Barry Philbin and Bobby Wonbon, Featherstone's Les Tonks and Keith Bridges – and all swopped punches as the trouble erupted. The Featherstone coach, Peter Fox, was furious when one of his players complained of a jaw injury and wanted to come off. Fox, claimed the Warrington camp, ordered his man to go back on and was told, 'We've lost the match and the fight. I'm coming off.'

Mike Nicholas remembers the final only too well: 'I was double-tackled and took a punch on the jaw. The game became a running battle.' Nicholas was to pay a heavy price. A broken jaw and knee ligament damage forced him to pull out of the forthcoming tour of Australia and New Zealand and robbed him of his Great Britain place. Murphy reflects: 'We had no shortage of hard men in our side. Featherstone picked the wrong day to find out. Mike Nicholas was a very hard man but broke his jaw and damaged his knee. Even hard men get hurt in this game. But you don't hear them scream.' Nobby Clarke added: 'We won the match and the brawl, though I don't condone that part of it. AJ hated needles but had to have those five injections to kill the pain and get him back on the field. That was typical of AJ. He led by example.'

Warrington celebrated victory long into the night but were keen to return home and show off the Cup. For Murphy it was another big occasion when he'd been a winner. Three times before, with St Helens and once with Leigh, he'd sampled Challenge Cup victory at Wembley. And the thrill was still as great. And so the Cup-winners headed for home the day after the final, the team coach leaving the M6 northbound carriageway at a pre-arranged point to take them to Woolston, on the outskirts of Warrington. There they boarded the traditional open-top bus for the triumphant drive through the town and a civic reception at the Town Hall.

The route was thronged with an estimated 100,000 well-wishers, as police struggled to clear a way through for the bus. The town needed its heroes after years in the sporting doldrums. Now they had them and intended to mark the moment. One banner proclaimed: 'Alex Murphy for Mayor'; another, 'Murphy for Prime Minister'. If the claims were fantasy, the sentiments were real enough. Rugby League in the town had come a long way in a short time since the days when Ossie Davies and Brian Pitchford had taken control of the club; a long way since angry fans had pelted the Warrington directors with orange peel and cushions because of poor team performances. Now the whole rugby world knew that Warrington were kings, and celebrations lasted long into the night. The town belonged to Murphy and his players, if only temporarily, as Cup euphoria filled the air.

For Davies and Pitchford the winning of the 1974 Challenge Cup justified their unswerving belief in Murphy which they had sustained since that early summer of 1971. 'He told us then that it would probably take him four years to win major trophies for the club,' reflects Pitchford. 'He had beaten his own forecast by a year.' Moreover, within a week of that Wembley victory Murphy's gallant team was to bring even more glory to a club which by now was bursting with self-esteem. And already the Great Britain selectors had recognized the team's performances by naming three players, Mike Nicholas, John Bevan and Kevin Ashcroft for the forthcoming summer tour of Australia and New Zealand.

13
Anti-climax

As Cup euphoria faded, Murphy knew there was still one major hurdle to climb to complete the club's most successful season in its history. On the Saturday following the great Wembley victory – 18 May 1974 – the team met St Helens at Central Park, Wigan, in the Club Championship final (the equivalent of today's Premiership final) which, astonishingly, was to be Warrington's fifty-second game of that remarkable season.

It was surely asking too much of players who'd already given their all in a bruising, exhausting final at Wembley to lift themselves again for such a demanding encounter. Murphy was fully aware that Wembley had taken its toll. Mike Nicholas had withdrawn from the Great Britain tour with a broken jaw and knee ligament damage. Murphy himself still nursed his painful rib injury and other players were also under treatment for knocks taken in the final. Few people gave Warrington much hope of crowning their Challenge Cup victory by winning the Club Championship Trophy as well, especially with an injury-hit team. But the doubters reckoned without Murphy's compelling desire to win. His brilliance

116

inspired his injury-ravaged side to a sensational victory by a single point over his former club, St Helens.

Brian Pitchford could hardly believe the result: 'It was one of the greatest performances I've ever seen from a Warrington team. We all wondered how Murphy could possibly motivate the players again so soon after Wembley. But he did and played superbly well himself into the bargain.'

Warrington won 13–12, with the most nerve-stretching moments crammed into the closing two minutes. St Helens missed a last-gasp attempt at a drop-goal to save the match. But there was still drama to come. With seconds left, Billy Thompson, the referee, called for a scrum-down under the Warrington posts. It offered Saints one last throw of the dice if they could win vital possession. Warrington came away with the ball and held on until the final hooter for a memorable victory.

Pitchford thought he saw Murphy say something to Billy Thompson after the scrum and couldn't wait to ask him about it. 'Murphy told me he'd suggested to the referee that it would be unthinkable to lose the game so late by conceding a penalty in that position.' Did Murphy feed the scrum? 'I've often wondered since whether AJ offended at that scrum and made his remark to divert the referee's attention at the crucial moment. Within seconds the match was over. I've never been so relieved to see a game finish,' admits Pitchford. And so the curtain closed on a remarkable season with Warrington one point and one move ahead of the opposition. But Murphy's job could now only get harder with the fans thirsty for even more success. He had produced a hard act for himself to follow.

Warrington maintained a winning momentum with another single-point victory over Wigan in the Locker Cup charity game before the start of the 1974–75 season. After that game, Ossie Davies was moved to observe: 'Alex Murphy is one of the greatest Rugby League personalities of all time.'

But Warrington started their league season – Murphy's fourth in charge at Wilderspool – in sloppy fashion, taking just one point from the first four. The fans looked for some sign of the previous season's spark when the team visited Rochdale Hornets in the first round of the Lancashire Cup. The game produced sparks but ignited a situation which blew up in Murphy's face. Mike Nicholas, one of the team's Wembley heroes only four months earlier, was sent off and Warrington crashed out of the competition at the first hurdle. 'It was my first game back after breaking my jaw at Wembley,' recalls Nicholas. 'One of their players seemed to want some glory against us. I think it was because we were the Cup-holders and he wanted to make a name for himself. He hit me so I retaliated in no uncertain fashion and was sent off. I wasn't a hundred per cent fit and certainly wasn't in the mood that day.'

Murphy had now been in charge at Warrington for three and a half years and was still leading from the front. Paradoxically this angered some of his team-mates, fed up with being dubbed a "one-man team". Senior players asked Murphy to drop himself. He obliged for four games but was soon back in the action: 'I didn't let injury finish my playing career and I wasn't going to let the players tell me when to go either,' he recalls.

In December 1974 Warrington played in the BBC's Floodlit Trophy final on a mud-covered pitch at Salford's Willows ground. Astonishingly not a single point troubled the scorer. Derek Clarke remembers it as a marvellous game: 'The players turned in a superb show despite the conditions. And there wasn't a single nasty incident throughout the eighty minutes.' The referee, Billy Thompson, has a more humorous re-collection: 'It was indeed a marvellous final. The rain came down all night, making conditions terrible. But the players were magnificent and a credit to the game,' he remembers. As the players and officials trudged off at the end Murphy complimented Thompson: 'Well done, Billy. Great refereeing, that,' he told the surprised official.

Murphy was to change his tune in the following month's replay at Wilderspool when Salford won 10–5. Thompson takes up the story philosophically: 'Salford's Keith Fielding scored a try, then was tackled by a Warrington player as he grounded the ball. I gave Salford a penalty in front of the posts and that made it a seven-point try in effect.' After the game Thompson went into the Warrington lounge for a chat and a drink. A glass of champagne was thrust into his hand. He turned to thank his benefactor: 'It was Murph.' He told me, "I hope it chokes you." Funny, I was his hero in the first match at Salford: now I was a rotter,' smiles Thompson when he recalls the evening. Murphy had other problems on his mind and quickly forgot the Floodlit Cup-final disappointment. Barry Philbin and Mike Nicholas, two of Warrington's heroes at Wembley, were unhappy and transfer-listed. The Cup-winning team was now facing a break-up. Philbin had been troubled with a back problem and was unable to command a regular place in the side.

Murphy welcomed the first round of the Challenge Cup at home to Halifax as a chance to get the club buzzing again. Warrington coasted through, beating the Yorkshiremen 32–6 to set up a second round clash with Wigan. There was still some residual ill-feeling between the two clubs from the previous year's quarter-final when Warrington had won 10-6 in a game disfigured by running battles. Again the meeting turned into a brawl with three players sent off, but again Warrington came out on top 24–17. New Hunslet were beaten 23–3 in the quarter-finals and the Cup holders now found only Leeds blocking their path to a Wembley return. Again the town was gripped by cup fever as Leeds were overpowered 11–4 at Wigan's Central Park to give Warrington their return ticket to Wembley.

But at Wembley, on 10 May 1975, Warrington met the emerging champions, Widnes. Murphy's magic spell was about to be broken. Four times he'd been triumphant at Wembley; now in his first visit as a non-playing coach he was to taste the bitterness of defeat. Widnes won 14–7 to give Murphy's old St Helens and Great Britain friend, Vinty Karalius, a victorious swan song. After the final, Karalius quit the Widnes coaching job to concentrate on his business affairs.

Murphy was shell-shocked after that Cup-final defeat. Wembley had always been his happy hunting-ground and Warrington had lost a final he believed they should have won.

He kept asking himself: should I have played? Many good judges believed so. Brian Pitchford thought Murphy would have tipped the scales in Warrington's favour in what was a very closely fought final. 'He left himself out of the team. I believe we would have won if he'd played. He was still very fit and his class would have told against Widnes.'

Murphy had gambled on the fitness of key players and had lost out. The scrum-half, Parry Gordon, had flu during Cup-final week and was isolated from his team-mates. He was only declared fit on the morning of the big game. The loose forward, Barry Philbin, was having treatment for back trouble. Murphy's assistant coach, Tommy Grainey, remembers well the problems they had that week: 'Four of our players weren't a hundred per cent fit. They only started training two days before the final. Even so, we started well and led 5–0 but it turned out to be a real sickener when we lost. It might have been so different if Alex had picked himself.' Pitchford endorsed that view: 'Losing to Widnes was a real anti-climax after the euphoria of the previous year'.

Murphy's team was now beginning to break up. The hooker, Kevin Ashcroft, returned to Leigh as player-coach that summer, Dave Chisnall was transferred to Swinton, and Derek Whitehead, Bobby Wonbon and Parry Gordon retired or were soon to do so. However, Murphy had the chance to put a smile back on his face with one last appearance in the Warrington colours in his testimonial game against an England side. The referee for the match at Wilderspool was his old friend Billy Thompson.

Though Murphy and Thompson had been sparring partners for years, they had tremendous mutual respect for each other. It was to be wittily illustrated during the testimonial game. With ten minutes left the pair swopped jerseys, Thompson going into the three-quarters for Warrington and Murphy donning the referee's jersey and taking the whistle. It was a chance he couldn't let go. When Thompson dropped a goal, Murphy-fashion, referee Murphy argued it should be disallowed for a minor infringement. 'It was a superb drop-goal,' says Thompson, 'one Murphy would have been proud of.

When we were walking off the field after Murphy had blown for time he turned to me and said, "Billy, you've had a stinker."' Murphy laughs: 'I'd been waiting for years to get my own back on Billy.'

The 1975–76 season – Murphy's fifth in charge at Wilderspool – was a struggle for the team which now needed re-building. Murphy tried but failed to sign the Welsh Rugby Union star, Steve Fenwick, to boost performances. However, in February 1976 an easy first-round Challenge Cup victory over Leigh Miners was followed by a 17–4 win at New Hunslet. It meant a quarter-final against Widnes, the Cup holders who'd beaten Warrington in the previous year's final. Murphy was looking for revenge and a chance to put the fizz back in the club. But 13 March proved unlucky as Widnes moved into the semi-finals after a 6–0 victory. Rumours were now rife that Murphy was ready to leave the club. His romance with Warrington, which had reached such heights, was losing its sparkle. Irritated by the Widnes defeat in the Cup, Murphy couldn't resist firing back. When St Helens got through to the final against Widnes, Murphy made an outrageous promise to the rugby public: 'If Widnes win the Cup, I'll jump off Runcorn Bridge.'

Widnes fans responded with banners and thousands of car stickers carrying the defiant threat: 'Murphy will have to jump off Runcorn Bridge into the River Mersey.' St Helens fans countered on his behalf. Their banners and stickers promised: 'We'll save Murphy from the Mersey.' No life-jacket was required. St Helens beat Widnes comfortably 20–5 and Murphy and his prediction were home and dry.

In February of the following season, 1976–77, Murphy's six-year reign at Warrington reached its lowest ebb when the team was beaten at the first hurdle of the Challenge Cup, losing by just one point – 13–12 – to the holders, St Helens. It was to be another twelve months before he could afford a smile when Warrington beat Widnes in the John Player Trophy final. With Murphy once again amongst the trophies, that win made up for some of the disappointments of the previous two years. Many believed that it would spark a new

121

beginning for Murphy and Warrington. In fact it served only to signal the end of an era. Within weeks his seven-year reign ended by mutual consent when he joined Salford as coach, a move which almost broke his relationship with two of his closest friends.

Albert White, his Warrington scout, whom Murphy had invited to join him at Wilderspool several seasons earlier, had been made an attractive offer to re-join Salford. The offer to White included a Salford directorship and full control of the scouting system at the Willows. 'It was an offer I couldn't refuse,' he remembers. White asked for time to think it over and then said he would accept if Murphy was appointed to the coaching job. 'The job's his,' was the immediate reply from a Salford board eager for Murphy's services.

White could scarcely wait to tell his friend of these developments. That night, after Warrington's training session, he was in the club lounge waiting eagerly for Murphy to arrive so that he could break the news. He was in for a rude awakening. Murphy unknown to White, had heard rumours that White was leaving Warrington for Salford and felt his friend had gone behind his back. White beckoned to his friend as he saw him enter the club lounge and asked him if he would like a drink, intending to reveal the news of Salford. He was not allowed to get the words out. 'Alex said, "I want nothing off you. Stick your drink." He was shaking with rage and shouting at me. I couldn't believe what was happening. He tried to order me out of the club. I decided I wouldn't enlighten him about Salford there and then. I also reminded him that he couldn't order me out of the club lounge because I worked for the company that owned the bar.'

Warrington's chairman had now arrived in the lounge and White told him of the Salford offer. 'Ossie Davies took off his glasses and cleaned them slowly. He always did that when he wanted time to think. He then said to me, "Anything Salford have offered I will offer the same."'

White left for home unable to understand Murphy's outburst but content to let him cool down. Next day he arranged to meet Murphy at the Millstone pub in Newton-le-Willows for a confidential chat. White put his cards on the table. 'Let's get it straight,' he told Murphy. 'If the chairman of a club like Salford approaches me, it doesn't mean that I'm walking out on you or Warrington. I've told them I won't take the job unless you become coach.' The air was cleared and the two men decided that they would link up at the Willows.

Murphy's appointment as Salford coach was made public in the week following the 1978 Cup final, when Leeds beat St Helens. Murphy and his wife Alice had accompanied Brian Pitchford and his wife Carol to the final and later had dinner at the Savoy Hotel. Murphy was nursing a misunderstanding and kept quiet about the Salford job. It was the first time in his seven years at Warrington that he'd hurt the feelings of his friend. 'We had always been honest with each other', Pitchford recalls. 'Unfortunately AJ had believed rumours that we were planning to part company with him. He'd been told we were not renewing his contract. I hadn't heard the rumours, but in any case they were untrue. Murph was also bothered about rumours that Ossie Davies and myself were fed up and planning to leave the club. It was all nonsense but was obviously bothering him.'

Pitchford remembers that over dinner Murphy was quieter than normal but didn't feel there was any significance in that. 'We had a splendid evening. An excellent meal and a chat over a few drinks. We all enjoyed it. The following week I was stunned when AJ handed in his resignation letter. If he had said something to me at the Savoy about his fears I could have told him what was really happening. I knew Ossie was finishing at the club and I knew I would be taking over as chairman. I could have told AJ at the Savoy that I wasn't intending to leave the club. The sad part of it all was AJ thought I was leaving and was bitter that I hadn't let him in on the secret. But it was pure rumour because I was certainly staying.' Murphy realized later that he'd made a mistake: 'I didn't have the bottle to tackle Brian Pitchford about it at the Savoy.' But despite this serious misunderstanding, the two men remained friends.

14
Champions

In the 1930s Salford Rugby League Club had toured the south of France and made such an impact that they were thereafter called *les diables rouge* – the Red Devils. They had enjoyed another period of ascendency in the 1960s and early 1970s under the chairmanship of Brian Snape, but had long since fallen on less successful days. It was hoped that Murphy's appointment as coach in 1978 would bring back some of the fire of the earlier period.

During a Warrington-Widnes game while Murphy was still at Wilderspool, players on both sides had started fighting as they walked off the pitch into the tunnel to get to the dressing-rooms. 'It became known as the "tunnel of love",' laughs Murphy's old friend, Albert White. 'Reggie Bowden jumped on Alex in the tunnel and the next minute the players were fighting.' Murphy had to face a disciplinary hearing, held at Salford, over the brawl and was fined £280 for bringing the game into disrepute. He was accused of pushing over the referee, Fred Lindop, in the tunnel, though Murphy vehement-ly denied the charge. 'Reggie Bowden pushed me and the players fell on top of Lindop,' was Murphy's recollection of events. After the disciplinary hearing White was asked to talk to the Salford chairman about the possibility of his returning to the Willows but instead he left with his friends Murphy and Maurice Lindsay, at that time a regular visitor to the Willows, who had brought Murphy to the disciplinary meeting in his sports car. Later the same month Salford approached White again and 'made me an offer I couldn't refuse'. The offer also included Murphy's appointment as Salford coach.

On his first day in overall charge of coaching at the Willows, Murphy fired warning shots at the Salford players: 'We will no longer be known as the "quality-street gang"', he said, referring to the nickname the team had been given as it slipped down the league. White recalls that first meeting: 'The Salford players hadn't been used to pressure because they had been working under Colin Dixon and Chris Hesketh who were only caretaker-coaches. Alex told the players he wouldn't ask them to do anything he couldn't do himself in training. But he warned them straightaway that he wouldn't tolerate them being late for training and he would not allow them to arrive untidily dressed. He told them they must be smart and clean whenever they represented the club. 'Murphy has always been a stickler for smartness of appearance,' White remembers, recalling the other advice Murphy offered his players: 'I want no excuses for missing training. No faked injuries, girl-friends' birthdays, mothers-in-law not well and their shopping needing to be done. Don't try any of these excuses on me because they won't wash.'

Murphy's new disciplinary approach was tested within weeks of his arrival. Salford were losing at home and at half-time Murphy, dressed immaculately in a cream raincoat, stormed into the dressing-room to confront the team. 'He told Harold Henney to buck up his ideas or he'd be thrown out of the club. Henney took off his mud-splattered shirt and threw it at Murphy. Mud dripped down his cream raincoat,' recalls White. White intervened quickly in the potentially explosive situation. He asked the other players to go back onto the pitch and warned Henney that if he didn't put the jersey back on and go on playing in the match he would never play for the club again. Henney went back out for the second half, Salford won and the incident was never mentioned again.

Early in his first season at Salford Murphy was asked by a group of American businessmen to coach Rugby League in the States. For a time it was rumoured that he was about to leave for America but Murphy was enjoying his new challenge at Salford despite the fact that his first season there ended in a relegation dog-fight. The following season Murphy's team beat his former club, St Helens, Salford's first victory over Saints in twelve attempts. It was followed by victory at Castleford in the quarter-finals of the John Player Trophy, and with Salford top of the league Murphy was named coach- of-the-month. But he was to be brought down to earth when Salford were beaten by Widnes in the Trophy semi-finals.

In January 1980 a 25–0 thrashing of Huyton away in the first round of the Challenge Cup saw Salford back in form. Rochdale Hornets were overcome in the next round to set up a quarter-final clash with Widnes. But there was again to be disappointment as Widnes beat them 9–8 with a drop-goal seven minutes from time in a marvellous match.

Murphy's second season of coaching at Salford had brought considerable improvement but only limited success. The team had reached the semi-finals of the John Player Trophy, the quarter-finals of the Challenge Cup and a top-four place. For Murphy, though, it wasn't enough. For the first time in his career he was not enjoying his rugby. For many reasons Salford was going wrong for him. In November 1980 soon after the start of his third season with the club, Salford played a re-arranged fixture at Wakefield Trinity. In a moment of pure theatre bordering on fantasy Murphy quit his job at half-time. Just two and a half years after taking charge at Salford with such high hopes, he was now out of work.

Some people thought Murphy's dramatic act had merely cheated the hangman. But even if the executioner had been waiting in the wings Murphy had been thinking long and hard about packing it in. On the day of the Wakefield game Murphy was unable to field his strongest team because of injuries. The problems seemed mountainous as he sat in the Salford dug-out watching his team struggle. With him was his injured skipper, Frank Wilson. Murphy handed Wilson a note and asked him to take it to the Salford directors' box in the stand. It was his letter of resignation, the final act in his Salford career which had been beset by problems from the start. Though he had enjoyed limited success at the Willows for once Murphy's magic had failed to inspire. Did his dramatic act of resignation at half-time in the Wakefield game really beat the hangman's noose as some of his critics believed? Or was his departure Salford's loss? Who can say? On the afternoon of Murphy's resignation his friend Albert White was a few miles away, watching a Rugby Union game. When White arrived home later that evening he was told by his wife, Rita, that the Salford chairman wanted him to telephone him as soon as possible. 'When I rang, the chairman said, "Your mate has quit. Frank Wilson gave me his resignation letter at half-time and I accepted it". Murphy had come to my home on a previous occasion, in fact when I was in bed with flu, with a letter of resignation and I tore it up. But there was nothing I could do on this occasion. He knew I would have tried to stop him leaving.'

White reflected on the high hopes the pair had had when they arrived at the Willows from Warrington. 'I've known Alex since he was a schoolboy. He was the best rugby player I ever saw. He was brilliant. He was a superb trainer and he always impressed you with his cleanliness and smartness of dress. I've heard him tell off players for having their socks round their ankles. He used to say to them, "If you're not a good footballer at least try to look like one." Not every player liked it. But Alex had high standards. He didn't have too much success at Salford though he got close. He had his enemies too. But it wasn't entirely his fault. Many of our best players were coming to the end of their careers.'

Some of the Salford players had been unable to take Murphy's demanding approach and even threatened to go on strike. On one occasion the players had complained to the club chairman about Murphy's approach, and a meeting was arranged and held in the banqueting-suite at the Willows with the club directors and Murphy facing the players about their grievances. The Great Britain scrum-half, Steve Nash, was the spokesman. Complaints against Murphy included harsh treatment, swearing and the way they were spoken to generally. Plenty of steam was let off at the meeting. White advised his friend not to lose his temper. ' "Keep cool," I told him, and he did. When the players had let off steam the strike threat ended.'

Within forty-eight hours of quitting his job at Salford, Murphy was in the crowd at his former club, Leigh, watching the Kiwi tourists. His arrival at Hilton Park for the New Zealand game sparked immediate speculation that he was about to return to the club he had led to their dramatic Cup-final victory over Leeds in 1971 when Syd Hynes was the first player ever to be sent off at Wembley. The Leigh secretary, John Stringer, tried to quell the rumours of an intended Murphy return by dismissing the reports as 'rubbish'.

However, Murphy was headline news again within sixteen days when the local paper declared, 'King Alex to Return.' Before the end of November – the month he had quit Salford – Murphy and the Leigh chairman, Brian Bowman, had agreed to shake hands on a three-year contract, making Murphy the new coach at Hilton Park. So Leigh and Murphy linked up for a second time.

Leigh's loyal fans gave Murphy a standing ovation when he was introduced to them before his first game back – a 24–8 victory over Barrow. But there were problems ahead. The former coach, Tom Grainey, threatened legal action against the club, and rumour and speculation began again as Murphy's name was suddenly linked with Wigan. However, in October 1981, Leigh beat Widnes at Central Park to lift the Lancashire Cup, Leigh's first trophy for ten years. That Cup win began a surge up the championship table as Leigh hit stunning form. When they beat Wigan 18–15 at Central Park in February it was their twelfth successive win – their best winning sequence since the end of the second world war. Then came the shock defeat by Castleford in the Challenge Cup quarter-finals and Murphy was carpeted by the authorities after criticizing the referee, his old antagonist Billy Thompson, for his handling of the game.

Then Easter defeats for the league leaders, Widnes, by Warrington and St Helens, and Leigh's own victories over Hull KR and Whitehaven, suddenly opened the door for Leigh to snatch the title, their first championship title for seventy-six years.

Murphy believed that that title win had proved to the doubters that he was a top-class coach in his own right when not playing. 'It's the proudest moment of my life,' he said, after winning the title. However, the championship win sparked off fresh speculation about his future. He admitted Wigan and his former club St Helens had made him lucrative job-offers. 'I'm happy to stay at Leigh,' he confirmed. But the pull of a new challenge was loosening his resolve to stay at Hilton Park, and representatives of both Wigan and St Helens went to his bungalow in Bold on a warm summer night in May 1982.

Eventually Wigan and Murphy's old friend, Maurice Lindsay, emerged triumphant as Murphy agreed to go to Central Park. Murphy's departure for Wigan was a bitter pill for his friend, Brian Bowman, the Leigh chairman. When he was told by Murphy that Wigan had made a positive approach, Bowman called an emergency meeting of his directors and invited Murphy to attend. He was offered an improved four-year contract by Bowman who, when he realized that Murphy was not to be tempted, said bitterly: 'I've been let down twice by Murphy. Once as a supporter in 1971 when Alex left to join Warrington and now this time as chairman of the club.' Murphy tried to alleviate his friend's anguish in a resignation letter he made public. In the letter Murphy explained how he had agonized over his decision to join Wigan but simply could not resist the new challenge that Central Park offered him. 'Leigh has been like a home to me and I have tremendous memories of both you and the lads,' he wrote to Bowman. Murphy went on to explain that his first coach and hero as a teenager at St Helens was Jim Sullivan, the former Wigan coach. 'I can't help feeling he would have wanted me to follow his footsteps. You know how I felt about Jim. I am feeling a bit low at the moment but I certainly hope that in time you will not think too badly of me.'

Bowman found little comfort in the Murphy letter. He recalled how the two of them had shaken hands on a new contract and he firmly believed that he had persuaded Murphy to stay on at Hilton Park to keep Leigh at the top. 'The new contract we had drawn up for Alex only needed rubber-stamping at the club's solicitors. Then I got a telephone call from our secretary, John Stringer, who told me Murph had signed for Wigan. I said to Stringer, "You must be joking?" I was so shocked by the news.'

Bowman faced up to the reality of the situation when his opposite number at Wigan, Jack Hilton, called at his office. 'Jack Hilton's a gentleman but I said to him "All the best, Jack. Here we are, these go with Alex" – and I gave him a bottle of valium tablets.' But despite everything, Bowman remains a close friend of Murphy and indeed was to link up with him again for a third spell at Leigh some years later.

Bowman's admiration of Murphy's outstanding rugby talent had grown over the years from the day when Bowman first watched him as a player at St Helens, and it was Bowman who had sounded out Murphy when he was locked in his bitter dispute with Harry Cook and his directors. Leigh's millionaire chairman, Jack Rubin, had asked Bowman to call at the Murphy home to talk to him about the possibility of him joining Leigh. That was the first step in a sequence of events which led eventually to the end of the deadlock between Murphy and St Helens and to Murphy and his family abandoning plans to emigrate to Australia.

Five years later, in 1971, when Murphy left Leigh for Warrington so dramatically, it was Bowman again who fired the first shots of criticism at the Leigh directors for allowing Murphy to leave. Bowman was at the forefront of the heated debate which split Leigh public opinion and caused uproar in the boardroom. A decade later Bowman himself was in the firing line as Murphy left again for Wigan. On that occasion Leigh took legal action and finished up £250 out of pocket when a top barrister advised them that they had no case. 'We couldn't prove any financial loss when Alex went to Wigan and because of that we were advised to drop the matter,' Bowman remembers.

The strain of the upheaval caused by Murphy's departure on that occasion took its toll personally on Bowman. 'Alex is a very hard man to work with but he compensates with the success he brings. And believe me there is no one who can bring success like Alex Murphy. For every hour of sadness he brought me at Leigh, he also won me much happiness. My happiest moment of all was in 1982 when Alex brought the club its first title win for seventy-six years. For me that was the greatest achievement in the history of Leigh Rugby League club. Winning the Challenge Cup in 1971 was obviously a tremendous achievement but when we won the championship that was our greatest moment. You have to be consistent over a whole season to win that title. It was a proud moment for me. I can honestly tell you I was a very happy chairman then and it was all down to Alex.'

Bowman knew that a working relationship with Murphy could be like living on the side of an active volcano. Eruptions were frequent as Murphy launched verbal rockets, delivered scathing opinions on players and directors alike, and breathed fire into the corridors of power at Leigh. But Bowman also knew of the compensations that would come with a full trophy room and Murphy's flashing wit offered him a soothing palliative when the heat was on. Bowman remembers the time he went with Salford's coach, Griff Jenkins, to watch the Glengarth Sevens tournament at nearby Stockport with some of the best Union players in the country taking part. 'I remember David Watkins scoring around a dozen tries in an absolutely marvellous display. He was good to watch and I couldn't wait to tell Alex. The following Tuesday I was watching Leigh having a training session and told Murphy about Watkins. I said to him "I've seen the·finest half-back playing rugby," and he said, "Pal, you're talking to him." I just burst out laughing.'

On another occasion Bowman was to catch another of Murphy's verbal rockets when Leigh were playing at Castleford in the John Player Special Trophy competition. Murphy himself had decided to travel ahead of the team to watch a Leigh Colts match at Featherstone Rovers and arranged to meet the Leigh team at Castleford half an hour before the scheduled kick-off. 'We arrived at the Castleford ground on the team coach ten minutes late and Murphy was there waiting for us. He absolutely blew his top. He told the players to wait outside the dressing-room but asked me and his assistant, Colin Clarke, to go inside with him. He was furious and blasted us both for being late. I tried to explain that we had stopped on the journey for a cup of tea but that only made matters worse. He told us in no uncertain terms that he wouldn't put up with people being late. When Alex spoke, everyone jumped, including me, the chairman. But I was prepared to put up with it because of the success Alex was bringing to the club.'

Despite everything Bowman lionized Murphy whom he considered not just a coach but a personal friend. 'Alex never bore grudges and you could never get to hate him. He's a wonderful character and for me the greatest personality in the game. Who can compare with Alex in Rugby League? He opens his mouth and says what he thinks to chairmen and directors alike but that's his way. You always knew there would be an end-product because he gets success. And let me tell you straightaway it's nothing to do with luck. He has achieved too much for that to be the case.'

Still, Murphy's unpredictability left Bowman speechless on many occasions. When Leigh lost a cup match at Hilton Park there was a major row between Murphy and the referee, Billy Thompson. 'I pleaded with Billy not to report Alex,' remembers Bowman. 'I asked Murphy to apologize or he would land himself and the club in trouble and he agreed. But when he went into the referee's room he blew up again. Fortunately I managed to smooth things over with Billy in a local hotel over a chat and a drink.'

That was not the only time that Murphy side-stepped his chairman when referee Thompson was involved. Bowman remembers clearly the April night when he was attending a testimonial dinner for Thompson at a hotel in Huddersfield and was sitting at the top table with Murphy. 'Alex turned to me and said, "Chairman, it's my birthday in ten minutes. Would you like to celebrate with me over a bottle of champagne at midnight?" I was delighted and Alex called over the waitress and asked her to bring us a bottle of the best champagne. The trouble was that he then moved three tables away and when the waitress returned with the bottle of champers I had to give her the money. She asked for £18 and I gave her twenty and left the table to go to the cloakroom. When I came back I asked our secretary, John Stringer, if she'd left me the £2 change. He told me that Alex had told the girl to keep it as a tip,' Bowman laughs.

There was more Murphy fun in a game at Hull Kingston Rovers. 'Alex had a clash with Rovers' loose forward, Frank Foster, and the referee called the two captains together and warned them to cool down. Murphy said to him, "What about their captain, ref?" Foster snapped back, "I am their captain," and Murphy replied, "and a bad 'un too." '

'We used to pay Murphy's telephone bill at Leigh and on one occassion he gave us his electricity bill as well. When we queried the electricity bill he asked us if we wanted him to ring people in the dark. You couldn't win with his wit so we paid the bills for him. I let him get away with things like that because he was a hero in the town. He was a living legend and was bringing success back to us,' Bowman admits.

Bowman's admiration for Murphy is undiminished though he frequently found himself so infuriated he had to reach for a sedative. 'He's a law unto himself and has never been any different. I remember going with the club to the 1971 Cup final and a group of us went with Alex for a visit to Petticoat Lane. We came across some of the Leeds players who were also out sightseeing and Murphy shouted to them, "Keep moving lads, they're stock-taking." He never missed a chance to score a point on or off the field. Even in Bowman and Leigh's finest hour, when Murphy took the club to its first championship success, he left Bowman in despair when he failed to catch the open-top bus for its celebration tour of the town. Murphy eventually caught up with the bus in the town centre, having been given a lift by his friend, Maurice Lindsay, then the Wigan vice-chairman.

'Murphy got out of the car and ran on to the bus and suddenly sat next to me,' Bowman remembers. 'I was astonished. But he's a one-off and always takes you by surprise. But what can you do with his track record. You have to put up with him if you want to succeed. Even now he's the only man, in my opinion, who could help us beat the Australians but he's offended too many people on the way and won't be given the chance again.' For all Murphy's demands on himself and everyone around him he was also to pay a personal price which momentarily threatened his career. 'We were playing Wigan in a cup-tie and Alex had chest pains before the match. Later a specialist examined him and told him he could have heart problems and ordered him straight to bed for a complete rest. I remember he was out of the game for a while but refused to let it get the better of him and within a short while he was back with his old bounce and confidence,' says Bowman.

'Alex was just as strict with himself as with his players. You paid him for twenty minutes work a week – the ten minutes before a match and the ten minutes at half-time. That's when Alex put everything into his work. I have never been in a dressing-room with anyone like him. He could pin point the strengths and weaknesses of the opposition in detail and with amazing accuracy. As a motivator he was the master and still is.'

It was no surprise to Murphy's friends that he would one day link up with Maurice Lindsay at Wigan. The two men had often discussed the possibility in their regular meetings over a drink and a chat. The friends used to visit local sauna baths and meet socially elsewhere. The night in 1982 when Lindsay finally persuaded his friend that it was time for him to join him at Wigan was an evening Murphy recalls vividly.

Two St Helens directors had already been to his bungalow home earlier the same night urging him to return to Knowsley Road. They said that the time was now right for him to help heal the wounds which had caused him to leave St Helens in bitter circumstances sixteen years before. Now the two Saints directors wanted him to forgive and forget. It aroused in him powerful loyalties as he recalled his teenage days at Knowsley Road where his career had started. Murphy shook hands with the two Saints directors when they left his home and promised to give them an answer the following day after sleeping on their offer. But his mind was practically made up already. Murphy was going back to his home town club where his father had taken him as a boy to sign professional forms.

Suddenly his thoughts were interrupted by a ring on the doorbell. 'When I opened the door I was staggered. Standing in the doorway were Jack Hilton and Maurice Lindsay. I can't remember which of them said, "Hello, Alex, we've come to talk to you about a job at Wigan." ' Murphy invited the two men into his home and soon all three were deep in conversation.

The Wigan coaching vacancy had arisen a few weeks earlier when the club had sacked Maurice Bamford after only one season in charge at Central Park. Bamford, who had succeeded George Fairbairn, the former player-coach, when Wigan were promoted back to the first division, and was later to become Great Britain coach, was stunned at the club's decision after just one season. He had kept his promise to hold Wigan in the first division and believed he should have been given at least another season to improve the club's position. He was heartbroken and said so. Now Murphy was being sought as his successor.

'Lindsay had wanted me to replace Fairbairn as coach before they appointed Bamford but he told me that the other directors had blocked the move,' recalls Murphy. The arrival of Jack Hilton and Maurice Lindsay at his bungalow home late that summer night had taken Murphy by surprise. But he liked what they were offering, and his earlier resolve to return to his native St Helens was weakening by the minute as Hilton and Lindsay spelled out what they were proposing. 'Lindsay offered me complete control of team affairs if I would join him at Wigan. He told me the directors would look after the business side of affairs at the club and that I would be in sole charge of team affairs, including the buying and selling of players. 'Don't worry about anything, Alex," he said to me, "we'll run the club and you can run the team."' Murphy warmed to the theme. He needed no more convincing when Lindsay said, 'Come on, Alex, join us at Wigan and together we'll make it a great club again.'

So Murphy became the highest-paid coach in the game at the biggest club in the game. 'Lindsay's a very persuasive man. He's a good talker and a good listener. At the time everything seemed right. Now, of course, I look back with regret that I turned down St Helens. My heart's always been at Knowsley Road because I'm a Saints lad, born and bred, and started my career there. I just felt Wigan had more to offer and was a better challenge at the time.'

15
Friendship

The seeds of friendship between Alex Murphy and Maurice Lindsay had been planted in the early 1970s when Murphy was player-coach at Warrington. Lindsay was friendly with Barry and Mike Philbin, who played under Murphy then, and it was they who introduced him to Alex. 'I got on well with the Philbins and Alex,' says Lindsay. 'We liked each other's company and our friendship mushroomed over the next ten years into a very close and happy relationship. We shared confidences. I liked him a lot and I think he liked me. But he was not my introduction to Rugby League. I'd been a Rugby League fan from being a boy.'

Lindsay, whose home was in Horwich, attended grammar school in nearby Bolton. 'I remember 163 out of 600 boys came from Wigan and they were all passionately in love with rugby and got me into their life-style. I went to Central Park as a twelve-year-old from Horwich and watched Oldham slaughter Wigan when Oldham had a great side.' Lindsay also recalls that when he was an eighteen-year-old trainee accountant with little spare cash, he wanted to go to Wembley to watch Wigan playing Hull in the 1959 Challenge Cup final.

'I had no money to go to Wembley so I volunteered to work a week-end for British Rail, as it was possible to do in those days. I had to be at Wigan station at 4.30 in the morning as the train left at 6.45.

'I worked as the lad in the buffet car. The steward gave me a ticket for the final and I watched the game from the uncovered end. I remember seeing David Bolton go through for Wigan and the great Billy Boston scoring a try.'

When Murphy took Warrington back to Wembley in 1975 to defend the Cup, Maurice Lindsay went with him. 'I think that whetted his appetite,' reflects Murphy. Though the 1975 final proved a disappointment to all connected with Warrington after their defeat by Widnes, the two men remained close friends. When Murphy eventually left Warrington to become Salford's coach in 1978, Lindsay went with him to the Willows, Murphy introducing him to a member of the Salford staff as his 'best friend'.

During the 1978–79 season the Wigan supporters became increasingly unhappy at the club's lack of success. The rumblings of discontent echoed from the terraces through the board-room windows as the club prepared to announce a big cash loss. Murphy's old protector, Vinty Karalius, the former St Helens loose forward, who had toured down-under with Murphy, took the unusual step of facing the Wigan fans in a head-to-head confrontation at the club. Vinty, not a man to duck an issue, faced questions both frank and at times brutal about the team's demise. The air was temporarily cleared. But storm clouds gathered again on the horizon, and Wigan's directors were under extreme pressure.

In the late summer of 1979 Karalius quit after three years as coach at Central Park. He was reported to have said in a memorable comment: 'This is a sick club and I'm not the right doctor.' When Karalius's assistant, Peter Smethurst, walked out in support, another former St Helens player, Kel Coslett, took over. But Wigan's problems continued on and off the field and, when two of the club's directors – Ian Clift, later to become the Swinton chairman, and businessman Tom Bennett – also decided it was time to go for 'business reasons', something pretty drastic had to be done to kick the sleeping giant into life.

The Clift–Bennett resignations left two important vacancies on the ten-man Wigan board, led then by the chairman, Harry Gostellow, and the vice-chairman, Jack Hilton. Rumours began to circulate that a group of local businessmen, who wished to remain anonymous but who were keen Wigan supporters, wanted to inject hard cash into the club. Then, in a move as surprising to many as it was swift, the two board-room vacancies created by the departures of Clift and Bennett were dramatically filled. Maurice Lindsay, destined to become the club's chairman, and Jack Robinson were co-opted on to the board in April 1980. Both men were described as 'Rugby League stalwarts'. Lindsay, it was also pointed out, was a close friend of the Salford coach, Alex Murphy. Within weeks the season ended in relegation for Wigan and Coslett's departure. The international full-back, George Fairbairn, was named as the new player-coach to plan the club's swift return to the first division.

Wigan's board was now back to its full strength of ten men. But the struggle went on with the bank overdraft getting bigger. However, with Lindsay and Robinson now co-opted on to the board, both men underlined their determination to revive the club. They flew to South Africa in a bid to sign the Springbok Rugby Union stars, David Smith and Ray Mordt. And they paid the cost of the trip out of their own pockets. Though the journey bore no fruit, the point wasn't lost on the club's annual meeting when they returned.

Director Robinson was in forthright mood at that meeting when the board and the chairman, Harry Gostellow, came under fire. The meeting ended in shouts of 'Resign', and twenty-four hours later Jack Hilton took over the chair, with Lindsay elevated to vice-chairman.

In March 1981, Wigan were beaten at Huddersfield in a brawling match dubbed 'the battle of Fartown'. Within weeks, the Huddersfield coach, Maurice Bamford, replaced Fairbairn though the club had already regained their first division status. The Wigan board felt that more experience was needed in the top division, and Bamford's appointment would enable Fairbairn to concentrate on his outstanding ability as a player. However, Fairbairn didn't see it that way. He felt he should have been given a chance to coach the team at the highest level and told his bosses so.

Again Alex Murphy had been suggested as Fairbairn's probable successor and again the speculation had proved to be unfounded, though the insistent message was prophetic. The time was fast approaching when Murphy and Lindsay would be teaming up at Wigan. Through the following season Wigan clung to their first-division status, but for Bamford the writing was on the wall. Survival simply was not enough for Wigan and Bamford was sacked. He was heartbroken.

Bamford's departure fuelled fresh speculation about a successor. This time Murphy's name was left out. It looked like a case of twice bitten thrice shy for the speculators and, if that was the case, they were wrong yet again for in June 1982 Alex Murphy left his championship-winning team at Leigh to become the new manager-coach at Wigan. Murphy and Lindsay were finally in business together, working for the same club.

Leigh, outraged at losing their star coach in such a way, took legal advice. It was to prove costly and fruitless. Murphy's arrival at Wigan was greeted with reverence. Maurice Lindsay said it was one of the biggest moments in the history of the club, and Jack Hilton endorsed the view that the club now had the best coach in the world. In an atmosphere of high optimism. Murphy assembled his coaching team. The former international forward, Bill Ashurst, was brought in; Alan McInnes was recruited from Salford; and Wigan's former international hooker, Colin Clarke, was put in charge of the 'A' team. It looked a combination of outstanding strength.

Murphy's first season in charge at Wigan started quietly with victory at newly promoted Carlisle. His first big signing, Brian Juliff, from Wakefield Trinity, made his Wigan debut, with another newcomer, Jimmy Fairhurst, one of the substitutes. But team affairs were about to be overshadowed as the spotlight turned full beam once more on the Wigan board-room, where the biggest upheaval in the club's history was taking shape. On the one hand sat four men with a mission: the chairman, Jack Hilton, his vice-chairman, Maurice Lindsay, and their board-room colleagues, Tom Rathbone and Jack Robinson, offered to throw the club a lifeline of more than £100,000 if they could have full control. Facing them sat the six directors who made up the rest of the ten-man board and the club's shareholders, who had to make the final decision. Behind the new plan was an offer of special stock to raise £112,000, the full amount of which Messrs Hilton, Lindsay, Rathbone and Robinson were prepared to underwrite in the form of a loan. However, there was an important condition: before Lindsay and his colleagues would agree to underwrite this special stock offer they insisted that the other six directors should stand down.

In the first week of November 1982, over 500 Wigan shareholders packed into the Riverside Club at the ground to thrash out the proposed new dawn at Central Park. There was only one item on the agenda – whether or not to oppose the plan to issue special stock to raise £112,000 for the club. In the event, it was given a massive vote of confidence, following assurances that there were no ulterior motives in the plan other than the club's well-being and financial stability.

Murphy believed the plan would help to revive the club's fortunes and backed his friend Lindsay. Hilton, Lindsay, Robinson and Rathbone won the day, and within two months of the shareholders approving the new financial arrangements and with the board-room changes having taken place the team was winning cups again, Murphy leading them to success in the John Player Trophy against Leeds in January 1983.

At the end of April, Murphy and Lindsay were able to look back on Murphy's first season as coach with a good deal of satisfaction. The John Player Trophy was in the Wigan board-room and the team had demonstrated the club's improving fortunes with a top-four place. Lindsay concedes: 'Things were going well and the gates had gone up from 4,000 to around 7,000.'

Then, in his second season, Murphy guided the team back to

Wembley for the first time in fourteen years. Cup fever once again gripped Wigan and the town's cherry-and-white army of fans prepared to invade London. Sadly it proved a false dawn. Wigan's neighbours, Widnes, spoiled the party by beating them 19–6 in the Challenge Cup final, and Murphy was crestfallen. He didn't realize it then but it was the beginning of a summer of discontent for him, ending sensationally in his row with Maurice Lindsay and his sacking twenty-four hours later.

The build-up to the Wembley final had been a happy time for Murphy and his friend Lindsay: 'Maurice was very impressed by the set-up at our London hotel and the preparations for the big game. After we lost I told him we would be back the following year. Wigan were, and won. But I wasn't there. But it was I who had laid the foundations. When I look back, I think Lindsay was going behind my back, talking with players and doing deals himself without me knowing. He found he was enjoying the job and the publicity. But though I was told that I would be in control of buying and selling players when I joined, that didn't always happen.'

Maurice Lindsay remembers differently the sequence of events which led to the eventual break-up of his close relationship with Murphy. 'I freely admit that if you spend ten years with Alex Murphy you'll learn an awful lot about the game. I have shared his moments of despair and enjoyment, and his moments of anguish when he's been on thin ice at clubs in a managerial capacity both at Salford and at Wigan, and I have supported him when he simply needed a friend's support.'

Lindsay is stung by suggestions that his friendship with Murphy was designed to enhance his own knowledge of Rugby League. 'Alex was not my closest tutor. Jackie Edwards was that and he has always been a close friend of mine'. Edwards, whose son is Wigan's present captain, was himself a schoolboy half-back with Murphy. 'And it is unfair to say I stood by Alex only to learn the game. But of course there were things I learned from him that I would not have learned from anybody else. Alex has the uncanny knack of sizing up situations very quickly and is probably the best judge in the game of his own professional players. He could always tell you very quickly what was his best team, and he has always had the ability to pick the right side.'

Lindsay also recalls how happy he had been personally when his friend Murphy won the Lancashire Cup and the first-division title at Leigh before joining him at Wigan. 'I was very pleased for him. He was happy again at last after his miserable time at Salford.

'Alex knew that one day success would come at Wigan,' Lindsay points out. And he recalls how the move was made to offer Murphy the coaching job at Central Park. 'There was a vacancy for a coach at Wigan after Maurice Bamford left. There was a mood to "get Alex". I knew in my heart how difficult he could be to work with and that if he came it would inevitably result in a final bust-up and loss of friendship. Out of duty to the club as a director, because I'm a democrat, I went to see him and invited him to come to the club.'

However, Lindsay reveals that just before offering Murphy the job, Wigan had been close to securing the services of the former Wigan and Great Britain captain Douggie Laughton. But in the end, 'I went to Alex's home with Jack Hilton and we discussed financial terms. That was the night the deal was done.' However, among Murphy's inner circle of friends, Billy Bates, a local licensee, and Bunny, a former horse-racing man, who now worked for Bates, wondered if the mixture would prove too volatile.

16
The Sack

In the summer of 1984 Alex Murphy again made headline news. Rugby League's most controversial character was on the front pages after being sacked as team manager and coach by Wigan after a calamitous row with his long-standing friend and ally, Maurice Lindsay, the club's vice-chairman. A friendship which had been developed and nourished over a decade ended dramatically when the two men locked horns over a claim by Murphy that he should be paid working expenses during a pre-season charity event at Central Park.

The realization that he'd been sacked hit Murphy with the speed and force of a guillotine. 'When it sank in that I'd been fired, I realized there'd be no more team talks, no more banter with spekkies on match days, no more weekly training sessions,' Murphy remembers. 'The money wasn't the real issue as far as I was concerned. I was going to give it to charity anyway.' Murphy believed he should have been paid for working on the afternoon of the Wigan Summer Sevens tournament – an annual charity event held at the club to raise cash for deserving local causes. He still recalls that catastrophic weekend in August with anger and frustration.

Inwardly, Murphy was devastated by the club's decision to sack him but fierce pride held back his true feelings. He reflects grimly: 'I was thrown out on my ear over a few miserable pounds. Looking back I think it could have been a set-up job. I know one of the directors hated my guts and wanted me out.' Murphy's sense of injustice cut him so deeply at the time that he thought about quitting for good the game he'd loved since his schooldays.

Many times he has tried to rationalize the events which had such disastrous consequences for him. Often he has wondered if he was the victim of a power game. 'Lindsay's an ambitious man and a very good businessman. But he always wanted to be in charge of everything. I think he believed I took the limelight off him.' However, those claims are strongly refuted by Maurice Lindsay who believes Murphy and himself had been on a collision course for some time.

During that summer of 1984 Murphy had been on holiday with his family in the south of France and there was no sense of anything untoward when he returned to his duties at Central Park. He vowed privately that summer that he would build a team capable of returning to Wembley to avenge the Challenge Cup defeat by Widnes the previous May. But dreams of the 'twin towers' soon turned to a nightmare on the Sunday of the Summer Sevens.

The Wigan seven-a-side competition has always been a popular event with the knowledgeable Wigan rugby public. With less players on the field there was usually scope for a feast of running. Fans were rarely disappointed. Murphy was looking forward with boyish enthusiasm to the 1984 Sevens which he hoped would provide a springboard for the coming season. Of all the clubs taking part that afternoon the inclusion of his former club, Leigh, gave Murphy a special reason to be satisfied. Leigh had reacted to his second walk-out by returning invitations to take part in the 1982 and 1983 tournaments. Now, in 1984, Leigh had decided to let bygones be bygones and had accepted Wigan's invitation.

Murphy was delighted and was looking forward to an outstanding event with Wigan, the host club, flexing its muscles along with Leigh, Oldham, Blackpool, Warrington, Salford, Leeds and Swinton. Murphy, sun-tanned from his recent holiday in France, eagerly awaited the action as did his assistant coach, Alan McInnes, and the 'A' team coach, Colin Clarke. A decisive victory over Oldham in the opening match of the afternoon convinced Murphy that his team was on course to regain the Sevens trophy won the previous year by Widnes, and his confidence was justified when Wigan won the trophy after beating Blackpool Borough in the final. But there would be no victory party for Murphy that evening.

During the afternoon he had noticed one of the office secretaries paying out expenses. When he questioned her, Murphy was told there was no money for him. 'I was told that Maurice Lindsay had left instructions that I would not be getting any expenses because I was on the club's staff.' Angry and fuelled by his belief that he was entitled to payment for his afternoon's work, Murphy went in search of Lindsay. The two men came face to face in the club's offices next to the dressing-rooms. 'I said, "Let's forget anything extra for coaching expenses. I'll take the same money as the players are getting. But you're telling me I should work all afternoon and get nothing." Lindsay then called me a money-grabbing little b.....d and took a wad of notes from his pocket and offered to pay me. I jumped up and my knee caught the desk. The telephone fell into his lap. I said, "If that's your attitude you'd better find yourself a new coach." I turned away and the telephone hit me.' If Murphy felt there would be a cooling-down period he was in for a surprise.

Later the same evening the other directors asked him to report to the ground the following day. 'Lindsay had obviously put his two-pennyworth in,' says Murphy. The next morning, Monday 20 August 1984, Murphy left his bungalow home early for his meeting with the Wigan directors at Central Park. He noticed immediately that Lindsay was missing and he could tell by the serious expressions on the faces of the other directors that he was in for some serious talking. 'I thought I would be getting a good rollicking because of my row with Lindsay.'

He asked why Lindsay was missing. The reply shook him even further. He was told the vice-chairman had gone to hospital for a check up on sore eyes. Then the chairman, Jack Hilton, told him ominously: 'We can't have you hitting directors.' An incredulous Murphy gasped: 'So you believe Lindsay's story without even hearing my side of it?'

Murphy reminded his chairman and the other directors, Rathbone and Robinson, that Lindsay had sat with his wife Alice after their so-called fight the previous evening. 'He had a chat with my wife and was quite friendly. He never mentioned anything to her about the row. And he didn't say anything about having sore eyes.' Murphy's words were falling on deaf ears. 'I knew I was hung, drawn and quartered.' He had been summoned to the ground that morning to be told the consequences of his bust-up with Lindsay.

The poignancy of the situation slowly dawned on him. Jack Hilton was giving him the sack. 'You're joking,' Murphy blurted out. But the Wigan directors were completely serious, and threats of legal action effectively ended public debate on the matter.

In a guarded statement, Jack Hilton pointed out that Murphy had been given the reason for his sacking which the Wigan directors concluded was in the best interests of the club. Within days of Murphy's sacking the spotlight of speculation beamed onto a possible successor, with rumours strong that the new man could be an Australian. But those rumours were dispelled when Murphy's assistants, Alan McInnes and Colin Clarke, took over as joint coaches.

Maurice Lindsay also remembers the traumatic events of that summer afternoon. Packets of money, each containing £20, were being paid out by an office secretary, Mary. Teams knocked out in the early rounds of the tournament were entitled to collect their expenses and leave for home if they wished. The visiting coaches got travelling expenses of £20. But Alex was the coach of the host club.

'When I walked into the office I was in a happy, carefree mood. It was a sunny day and I was happy because Wigan had won. Alex flew into a tirade and asked if I thought he would work for nothing. I didn't know what he was talking about. I said, "For God's sake don't get upset for £20; I'll give it to you myself." He said, "*You'll* give me £20? You and your directors can stick this job up your ------," and that's when the telephone came across.

'I didn't call him a money grabbing little b.....d. I didn't get time to think. He blew up. When I got home that night I knew that our ten years of friendship had gone west.'

17
Always a Saint

After he had been sacked by Wigan, Murphy went out of the game he loved. Work as a radio and television commentator kept him in touch with the game until in 1985 Leigh offered him the hand of friendship for a third time. He couldn't prevent the team dropping into the second division from a hopeless position but when he left, several months later, they were almost unbeatable in the lower division and heading for promotion. Then, in the autumn of 1985 he was sensationally invited back by his first club, St Helens, twenty years after he'd left them in bitterness.

First, he asked his mother if he could return to Knowsley Road, so keeping a promise he'd made to his late father that he wouldn't return to St Helens if she didn't want him to. The man he'd been at loggerheads with all those years before, the St Helens chairman, Harry Cook, welcomed him back: 'When he came back to us, I was very happy.' Cook had finished as the game's longest-serving chairman some years before. He had tried on a previous occasion to bring Alex back to Knowsley Road but couldn't get unanimous backing from his fellow directors but he had always believed that one

149

day Alex would come home.

'Alex was a wonderful player. But we had many wonderful players when Alex first played for us, players like Vollenhoven and Karalius. Vinty Karalius looked after Alex. I remember going to Widnes one Boxing Day morning to sign a centre playing for the Widnes junior team. I told them to forget the centre, I wanted the loose forward. It was Vinty Karalius. I knew he was going to be a good player and I was proved right. He was a very strong man. I knew Alex would do the business with Leigh when he left us and with Warrington later on. He had a quality other people have not got. He can inspire people. If he could just curb his tongue, he'd be a perfect gentleman. Mind you, I think he's getting better as he gets older. I knew one day he would come back to St Helens. Knowsley Road is his grass roots. It's his home. Yes, he's a grand lad and I'm glad of my association with him. I expect he always wondered when we appointed other coaches, why we didn't approach him. He's still strong, still good at the game and still a good motivator. He's got to keep Saints at the top, and he will. He's still outspoken but he's good for Saints. I can't see him getting tired or his enthusiasm going for a long time yet. He'll bring the good days back.'

It was in 1985, shortly after Murphy's third return to Leigh, when Lancashire, coached by Murphy, were due to play the New Zealand tourists at Oldham's Watersheddings ground. The game was called off only minutes before the scheduled kick-off because the frozen pitch was considered too dangerous to play on. Within minutes St Helens had made the informal approach to Murphy which led to him returning to his original club. The St Helens chairman, Lawrie Prescott, and Joe Pickavance, a director, had been delegated to sound out Murphy who warmed to their invitation to 'come back home'. Within days he had replaced Billy Benyon as St Helens's coach – nearly twenty years after his embittered departure as their all-conquering captain. Harry Cook was delighted. 'I said to him, "Welcome home, Alex." He smiled and said back to me, "Thank you." We never speak about the past now. We let sleeping dogs lie.'

Needless to say, immediately on his return to St Helens, it was reported that some of the players had decided not to play under him as a coach. Murphy, never one to mince words, gave them the benefit of his advice: 'If anyone doesn't want to play for Alex Murphy, they can go now,' he said bluntly. No one did. But the rumours of dressing-room discontent became stronger as St Helens plunged to eight successive defeats in Murphy's new reign.

After one defeat by Bradford Northern, when St Helens collapsed after taking an early lead, Murphy laid down his law in brutally frank terms: 'This is the most humiliating Saints side I've ever seen,' he proclaimed. 'There are still rumours circulating that some of the players don't want to play for Alex Murphy. I'll tell them again they can go.' And he insisted that his chairman, Lawrie Prescott, should visit the dressing-room and give the board's view of the situation. Prescott confirmed to the players: 'We will get it right with or without you.' The players now realized that Murphy's word must be obeyed or they would have to accept the consequences and look for another club. The situation changed immediately, the team hit peak form and started a record-breaking run of victories.

Once the initial difficulties had been ironed out Murphy believed his talented squad needed only a couple of players to put the club back amongst the honours. Just before Christmas 1986, he had steered St Helens to the top of the league and the scene was set for a glorious Cup-run.

Swinton almost spoiled the party in the preliminary round at Knowsley Road when they had St Helens hanging on for a narrow 18–16 victory. Then, travelling to Yorkshire in the first round, Saints brushed aside Dewsbury 48–12. Next came Oldham, who had knocked out the Cup favourites Wigan in the first round. Murphy's team triumphed again at the Watersheddings by 24–14 to set up a quarter-final against Whitehaven at home. Another convincing victory by 41–12 over the Cumbrians put Saints through to a semi-final against Leigh at Central Park.

In a fiercely contested match St Helens beat Leigh 14–8, and Murphy was back at Wembley for a seventh time – twenty-six years after he'd first been there as a St Helens player. St Helens's Australian full-back, Phil Vievers, was the man-of-the-match in their semi-final win, but no Saints fan doubted the importance of winger Barry Ledger's try-saving tackle on John Henderson when the Leigh man looked a certain scorer with the line in front of his nose. So the 'twin towers' beckoned once more. Murphy would be back in town.

Just over a quarter of a century since the brilliant young Murphy had first helped St Helens to beat Wigan 12–6 at Wembley in the 1961 final, he was taking the club back for Rugby League's first million-pound gate. The big game started disastrously for St Helens. Halifax scored a try in the twelfth minute, and with the men from Knowsley Road lacking bite and fire the Yorkshire club eased into a 12–2 half-time lead.

During the break Murphy pulled no punches as he told his players what he expected from them in the second half. The magic worked almost immediately. Within a minute of the re-start, Murphy's New Zealand Test centre, Mark Elia, broke from his own 25-yard line, accelerated away as Halifax players tried to close in for the tackle, and headed for the try-line. Elia in full flight beat the Halifax full-back, Graham Eadie, the eventual man-of-the-match, on the outside to score a superb solo try and put Saints back in contention.

Halifax scored again to win back their 10-point cushion. Then John Pendlebury took a leaf from Murphy's book and dropped a goal. It was to prove a decisive kick. But once again St Helens hit back. Paul Round's try, converted by Paul Loughlin, narrowed the gap to just one point. Elia crossed the line for what appeared to be a certain match-winning try only to have the ball knocked from his grasp by Pendlebury before he could ground it. Murphy was despondent.

Elia's lapse apart, why had his players failed to produce a drop-goal in the closing minutes which would have levelled the score? This was a particular irritation to Murphy who had instructed his players in the skill of drop-kicking during his Wembley build-up. And of course it had been Murphy himself who had dropped a record five goals over three Wembley appearances – one with St Helens in 1966 and two more in each of the 1971 and 1974 finals when he played first with Leigh and then with Warrington.

Murphy's frustration exploded within seconds of the defeat by Halifax. He blasted the referee, John Holdsworth, and his assistant, Dave Chisnall, also clashed with the Halifax substitute, Brian Juliff. But for Murphy, the only player to captain three different winning teams at Wembley – St Helens, Leigh and Warrington – that 1987 final was the one that got away.

However, eight months later – in January 1988 – Murphy brought smiles back to St Helens and another cup to the trophy board at Knowsley Road. This time it was through a single-point victory over Leeds, 15–14, in the John Player Trophy final to lay a seventeen-year jinx that had seen them fail to reach the final of that competition. The outstanding player in that win was the young centre, Paul Loughlin, whom Murphy had dropped earlier in the season with the warning, 'Pull up your socks or else.' The talented youngster had now repaid the club with interest.

Again Murphy had upset the odds, just as he had done in spectacular fashion in the 1971 Wembley final when as player-coach he led Leigh to a magnificent victory over Leeds. Before that final Murphy and a few friends had gone to a dog track in London for an evening's relaxation from the pressures of the big game. They backed six winners, taking over £2,000 off a bewildered bookmaker. 'I told the bookie that Leeds were about 5 to 1 on to beat us in the final, and suggested he should lay a book on Leeds and offer them at even money,' recalls Murphy. The bookie responded: 'With your sort of luck you could very well beat Leeds.' And so the bookie laid even money Leeds. 'The punters knocked him into the back of the stands, they were that eager to have a bet on Leeds and the bookie took £25,000 in bets. After we had beaten Leeds he brought two crates of champagne to our hotel. He couldn't believe what had happened.

Murphy was always a master at upsetting the odds and the opposition. His skills at kicking drop-goals helped to bring about a reduction in their value from two points to one. And he was responsible for another change in the rules when he used an offside tactic against Wigan in his 1966 Cup-final win. Wigan's regular hooker, Colin Clarke, had been suspended and they were forced to play another forward, Tom Woosey, with little experience of hooking, in that position. Murphy realized that if he was caught offside, then each penalty he conceded would in fact give possession back to Saints for in those days a scrum would follow a penalty-kick for touch. Murphy, knowing that the St Helens hooker, Bill Sayer, would almost invariably outhook Woosey, was content to concede a penalty, knowing that the resulting scrum would give Saints possession.

Murphy denies that he moved into offside positions deliberately to give penalties to Wigan though it certainly lead to Wigan being denied vital possession and left their international skipper, Eric Ashton, bemoaning Murphy's so-called 'offside tactics'. 'We were a fitter side and more versatile than Wigan,' was Murphy's counter-response.

In any event, the offside law was examined after the game and a year later changed – a change sanctioned by the International Board – to give a tap-penalty, rather than a scrum, against the offending side after ground had been gained by a kick for touch.

Murphy still has his eye firmly on winning the Challenge Cup in his own right as a coach. Three times now, in 1975 with Warrington, again in 1984 at Wigan, and in 1987 with St Helens, Murphy, never on the losing side as a player at Wembley, has tasted defeat as coach. 'I've won everything else as a coach. Perhaps when I lift the Cup, and I will, then the doubters will shut up,' he says defiantly.

18

The Greatest

Murphy has been the dominant force in British Rugby League for over three decades. He has captured the public's imagination from St Helens to Sydney, Perpignan to Papua New Guinea, Auckland to London, and always as the leading man. A hero and a legend from his teens, Murphy has been the inspiration for a generation of aspiring players needing a goal to aim for and someone to emulate. He has confronted opponents on the field with the same head of steam that he has challenged the law-makers off it, and if he could use the rule book to his own or team's advantage then tough luck on the opposition and the mandarins alike. For Murphy, laws are made to be challenged and tested in the manner of Jonathan Swift who likened them to cobwebs catching only small flies.

Paradoxically, Murphy holds many officials in high regard, even some who punished him for his indiscretions as a player. The first referee to give Murphy his marching orders was Eric Clay, known as the 'sergeant-major'. Despite the nick-name, Clay had served, like Murphy, in the Royal Air Force and gave Murphy his first sending-off for fighting in a St Helens game during the 1959-60 season. 'Eric Clay looked the wrong shape for a referee. He had a big belly but that could kid you. He knew how to handle men and I respected him. He looked like a sergeant-major and spoke like one and I pushed him as hard as I could but if he sent you off you knew it was a fair decision because he had no favourites', says Murphy.

The second occasion on which Murphy disputed the laws of the game with Clay was during another St Helens match, this time against Huddersfield, in the first round of the Challenge Cup when Murphy was a national serviceman in the RAF.

The St Helens Springbok winger, Tom Van Vollenhoven, had made a break and was 'stiff-armed' by Peter Ramsden. 'I was so annoyed that Voll hadn't passed the ball to me that I chased Ramsden and kicked him,' admits Murphy. After the game Aircraftman Murphy was still fuming about the Ramsden incident and spotted Eric Clay in the bar. 'I called him a fat Yorkshire b.....d and threatened to throw him across the car park. I think he objected strongly to the word "Yorkshire" because he reported me for that and I was banned for another two games for abusing him.' The two men clashed yet again when Murphy rounded on Clay during a game and told the referee he had no right to keep calling him 'yapper'. For once Murphy was temporarily stumped as Clay retorted, 'Sue me.' 'I admit I gave Eric Clay more lip than anyone else but he knew where to be on the field and was always in the right place to make a decision. That's why I respected him.'

Another top referee Murphy had his clashes with was Fred Lindop, the last official to send him off for a retaliation offence. 'He was a prima donna when he first started. He was a male model for clothing and I told him he should pack in refereeing and take up modelling full-time. But I grew to respect Fred a lot. I gave him stacks of abuse but he never took much notice. I have certainly had my battles with him but Lindop was a good 'un. I admit I was wrong at times but referees can also have their bad games. Some people think I hated the man but at St Helens he is invited into the board-room and stays for a drink.'

Murphy is also lavish in his praise for his old adversary Billy Thompson. 'I never won with Billy. I pulled the wool over his eyes a few times but he pulled it over mine a lot more. I used to get upset with Billy even when I was trying to be nice to him. But Billy didn't sulk. He was a man's man. And a very good referee.'

It was not always a referee who had to curb Murphy's excesses. Jack Meadows, later to become the St Helens kit man with Murphy, remembers his early days as an official when he was refereeing a schoolboy match in which the up-and-coming Murphy was playing. 'At half-time a priest who was watching the game asked me to have a word with the little lad wearing the number seven shirt because of his swearing. It was Murphy. When I told him what the priest had said, I didn't hear another word from him.'

If Murphy has been subject to the law throughout his career he has also been a law-maker himself. One of his firm rules has always been to insist that players under his charge should be clean, smart and punctual. 'If people are on time they're usually interested in what they are doing. It costs nothing to have a wash, comb your hair and be smart. I was brought up that way by my father. I remember he told me never to be late and warned me that being five minutes late for an interview could mean someone else landing a job before you.' His father's advice has been a guiding principle for Murphy throughout his professional career when dealing with players. And he has always practised what he has preached about personal appearance though his fellow pros have never realized how easy it is to knock him out of his stride. 'I hate people ruffling my hair. It's something that really angers me. If other players had known this and done it, it would have been the one thing to have knocked me off my game. But no one ever found out and I made sure they didn't.'

Murphy's 'clean and smart' law was put to the test when he was coach at Wigan and the team was preparing to leave for a match. The hooker, Nicky Kiss, arrived wearing sandals and a tie with a collarless shirt. 'I told him to go home, get changed and smarten himself up or he wouldn't be playing. We met him later at a motorway service station and he was dressed properly to represent the club. If he hadn't tidied himself I would have dropped him from the team for that game. I believe you should set a good example as a professional.' Murphy still makes the same demands on himself and his players though he admits that 'my bark's worse than my bite'.

Murphy's playing ability may have diminished but his fire and enthusiasm for Rugby League is as fierce as ever. He does not believe that Britain has produced any great players in recent seasons. 'We give international recognition and false price tags to players who wouldn't have got a game in a training session in my playing days,' he grumbles, recalling Britain's 1962 Ashes-winning Test team in Australia as the best players he has ever seen. Murphy of course, has his favourites like his St Helens and Great Britain friend Vinty Karalius. 'At loose forward or anywhere else Vinty was the hardest man I've ever seen on a rugby field,' says Murphy. 'He was called after three saints, Vincent, Peter and Patrick, and off the field he was a perfect gentleman. But on it – my God, he was fearful.' At full-back there would be Glyn Moses with Tom Van Vollenhoven and Billy Boston on the wings. Who could have caught or stopped either of those two in full flight!? In the half-backs would be Ray Price and Gerry Helme, with Alan Prescott, the man who played on with a broken arm to beat the Australians on the 1958 tour, also a certainty for Murphy's best-ever team. And Dick Huddart would be in it along with the British and Australian skippers, Eric Ashton and Reg Gasnier. Today Murphy is still hunting for new talent: 'You don't see the likes of Gareth Edwards and Barry John too often. They both had something special and would have made the grade in my game.'

Great Britain's selectors have always been a target for Murphy's advice especially when they select what he describes as 'ham and eggers' – ordinary players who go on tour, in his view, simply to make up the numbers. 'They only go for a sun tan with no real chance of making the Test team. I think they go because the old pals act still comes into it.' That again is Murphy firing on all cylinders just as he has done throughout his long career. The man whom a 1987 poll of players voted 'the coach most professional players dislike' won it by a mile.

'I've always been streets ahead of the bloody lot of 'em,' he replied when told the poll result.

The pollsters had merely aped the Lancashire selectors who, during Murphy's glorious reign at Leigh, had failed to find him a seconder when he was proposed for the team to meet Yorkshire in a county game at Salford. He responded with a man-of-the-match performance for Leigh in a club game the same week that Australia's Miss World, Penny Plummer, watched him. Not realising who he was, she told people sitting nearby in the stand, 'The chap with the number seven on his back stands on his own!' Nothing has changed.

The three R's for Murphy are rugby, rugby and more rugby. He could have been a successful soccer player or an outstanding golfer such was the range of his talent and athleticism. Rugby League has been the richer for being his first choice.

Will St Helens be the end of the road for Murphy? Before he returned to heal the twenty-year rift he had asked his mother if she would let him go back, thus honouring the old promise he had made to his father. Of course she did not stand in his way. 'I have never interfered with his life. But when he finishes at St Helens this time, I think that will be the end of his rugby career.' Murphy agrees. 'My next club will be the DHSS,' he laughs.

But don't bet on it.